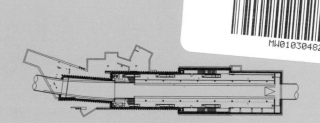
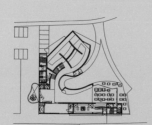
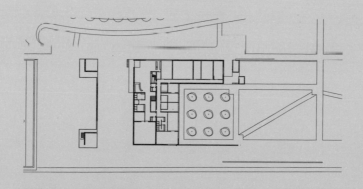
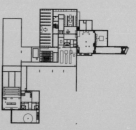
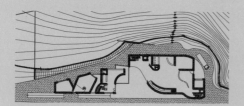
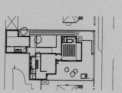
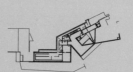
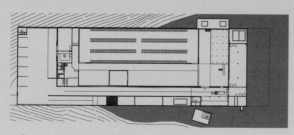
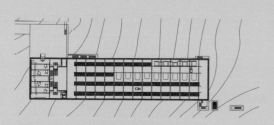
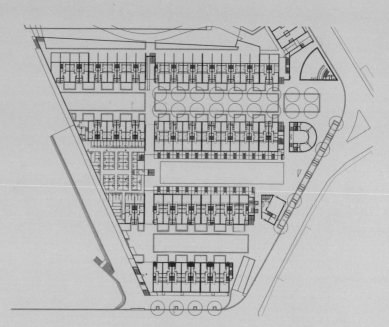

Álvaro Siza: The Function of Beauty

Álvaro Siza: The Function of Beauty

Álvaro Siza: The Function of Beauty

Carlos Castanheira

Introduction

Álvaro Siza has now reached the age of 75 and has completed 54 years of professional activity. His interest in building, or architectural construction, manifested itself early, when at about 15 years old he designed and built a shed in the garden of his parents' home, which served as workshop and study space for his brothers. The pavilion, as the family calls it, still exists and is soon to be restored. Next came the remodelling of the kitchen in his grandmother's house, followed by a gateway for an uncle, a bathroom for a family friend, four semi-detached houses, studying architecture at the School of Fine Arts in Porto, contact with the architectural master Carlos Ramos, travels abroad – in particular to Finland – and his work and friendship with Fernando Távora.

This learning process could be classified as natural for Siza, who seemed predestined to create works that are continually fresh and current, and that despite the passing of the years, sometimes many years, continue to be up to date. Siza's professional path is filled with projects that once started were not completed, with projects that were completed but never built, and also with finished buildings, many buildings, so many and so varied. Looking at the built work, it is easy to see its persistent quality, its lack of mannerisms and absence of trivial and passing fads. If we look at the unbuilt projects, we also find the same coherence and quality, together with perfect contemporaneity with the time of their conception. We would also recognize the waste of so much unjustifiably cancelled work and ask ourselves where would architecture be now if projects such as the building for Avenida da Ponte, Porto (1968–74), the house for Mário Bahia, Gondomar (1983–93), the pavilion for *Guernica* in Parque del Oeste, Madrid (1992), the landing quay in Thessaloniki (1996), the Kiasma Museum of Contemporary Art, Helsinki (1992–93), the remodelling of the Sala degli Scaloni in Castello Sforzesco, Milan, where Michelangelo's *Pietà Rondanini* is housed (1999), or the extension to the Stedelijk Museum, Amsterdam (1995–98) had been realized. Much changes during 75 years of life and 54 years of work, but Siza has always known how to reinterpret the new challenges to be faced, whether in small projects during his early days in practice, or the large projects that resulted from, initially, international and, only later, national recognition of his work. His first works abroad were not well received by the critics, who, at first, without much thought, were disappointed that Siza had not transferred his own design process to Berlin, The Hague and, later, other places. They thought Siza was being too restrained by the local context. What they wanted was for him to transplant abroad something that they already knew and liked. To take a risk on the familiar, and be made uncomfortable by the obviousness of the solutions and by the contemporary reinterpretation of what some call vernacular, seemed for some too banal.

Siza has got us used to being surprised. He is German when he works in Germany, Dutch in his projects for The Hague, Korean in Korea and Portuguese when he is allowed to be. He unsettles us with surprise, with evidence and above all with continual balance and quality. I have known Siza, without realizing it, since the time the Oliveira de Azeméis bank was being constructed (1971–74). I was attending the nearby secondary school and out of curiosity started to follow the construction of this new building. This was before the Revolution of 25 April 1974. Building at that time was not as it is now, particularly in a small town such as Oliveira de Azeméis. In those days a building went up only rarely and this particular building was strange right from the start. To be strange was something innovative and promising for a curious young man, in that almost stagnant environment, when generally something new was actually something second-hand.

I remember seeing a small group of people visiting the works and I remember seeing a man leading, explaining why particular decisions had been made. I know today that a decision is no more than a succession of persistent doubts, which becomes a decision, although the persistence of the doubt will remain as part of the search for perfection. The building was completed in 1974 and, despite the changes that have been made over the years, it remains today a contemporary building.

In 1976, I started my studies in architecture at the School of Fine Arts in Porto, the same school that Siza had attended and where he was teaching at the time. In common we had and have Fernando Távora as a teacher and ever-present friend. Already a student, I met Siza in 1976 and only then realized that he was the author of that strange and beautiful building that had been built shortly before, just beside my secondary school. Even then I was aware that there was already something differentiating him from the rest, not only in his attitude – which some refer to as distracted, which I now know to be attentiveness – but primarily in his buildings, of which there were not a large number at that time, and in the promise that his post-revolution projects already showed.

As a student, and later as an architect, I worked with Siza on many projects in Portugal, but primarily abroad. Some were built, others not, but they are all fresh: although some are 30 years old, some less, they are all young. 25 years ago I started to organize and curate exhibitions about the work of Siza and have never stopped. Nowadays these exhibitions are not only about architecture but also about other interests that Siza has been nurturing and has of late, despite his wide range of activity, been able to develop: furniture, design and sculpture. These aspirations were thwarted by the pressures of professional activity, but when allowed to grow have produced excellent results. Organizing, coordinating and producing exhibition material has allowed me, obliged me, to keep in touch, very closely, with Siza's work and to contemplate and write about some of his buildings.

This book is a compilation of projects that are currently under construction or that have been completed recently. It is a selection that is open to criticism, as is the decision to present the work through sketches, initial drawings with successive alterations, completed drawings, when possible, photographs of the building work in progress, written descriptions and, almost always, photographs of the completed buildings. These works will remain recent even when Siza comes to be 100 years old and continues to work with the same contemporaneity as he did 54 years ago, and with a persistent joviality. Such is timeless architecture. Such should be the architecture of our times. Such is the body of work of Álvaro Siza. Such does this book aspire to be.

– Carlos Castanheira

Bouça, Águas Férreas Cooperative
Porto, Portugal
1973–1978 / 2000–2006

Bouça, Águas Férreas Cooperative

The completion of Bouça was, for me, almost a surprise. After the 1974 Carnation Revolution in Portugal, an organization called SAAL (*Servicio de Apoio Ambulatorio Local*) was formed essentially as Portugal's government housing authority, and particularly encouraged local residents to organize their own building.

This housing was built as part of SAAL's programme, but by 1978, with about one-third of the designed housing blocks built, work on the project stopped. I never completely lost faith that it might be finished, particularly given the continuous pressure exercised by the residents of the incomplete houses of the first phase. And after almost 30 years, it was the commitment from the residents' Federation of Cooperatives that helped solidify the decision, by Porto's County Council and the National Institution for Housing, to complete the work.

This decision included a commitment to build the second phase as well as refurbish the existing houses. It proved difficult to convince some of the residents to do without a number of improvised interventions that had been added since the construction of the first phase. Despite the degradation of the construction, the residents felt they lived in 'magnificent isolation' in the centre of town. We understood their difficulty in accepting an interruption of this lifestyle, and also the fear of a possible increase in their rent.

A patient dialogue with the existing residents was necessary, in which our obligation to maintain the original project (with a few exceptions) became clear. Our determination was to preserve the already built and lived-in residences, and to include them with the new buildings in a unifying plan. Our dialogue yielded some compromise and some innovation.

I too was having some doubts and difficulties. The revision of the project forced me to look at the profound changes that had taken place in the attitudes of the project's population, a strong contrast to the context prior to the Revolution of 1974. The current necessity for a garage was previously unthinkable, as was the contemporary preoccupation with the demarcation of public and private space. It also would have been impossible to foresee the level of requirement demanded by current regulations.

Bouça was an economically radical project. In 1974, it could not – should not – have been anything else. But in discussing the project decades later, the wish (and the possibility, although slim) of providing for a higher level of quality and comfort became apparent. Now that the project is complete, the market's reaction shows that this type of dwelling does not fully correspond to contemporary expectations for affordable housing. But it is attractive to other sectors of the population, such as students, young professionals, and new families: protagonists in the mobility that characterizes the contemporary city.

In the revision to the project, the integrity of the original one is somewhat lost. But now there is an underground station right outside the door, a flow of people crossing the site, service buildings open to the surrounding streets, a well-kept garden, cars... just as in any housing scheme.

It isn't a perfect project. But is that the most important thing?

– Álvaro Siza

Siza's original sketches of the housing blocks.

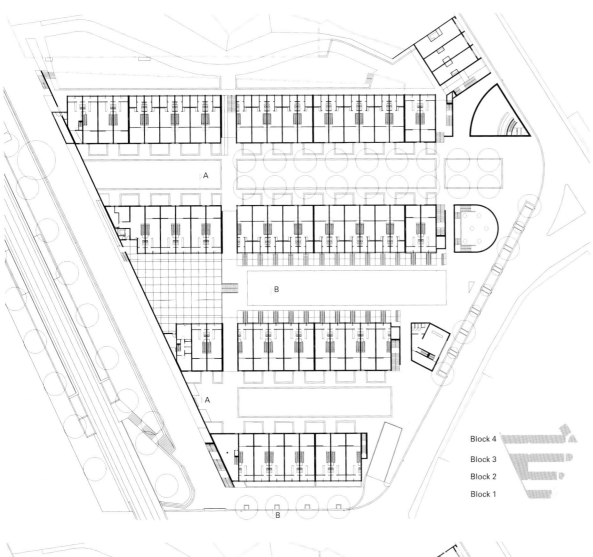

Block 4
Block 3
Block 2
Block 1

First-floor plan

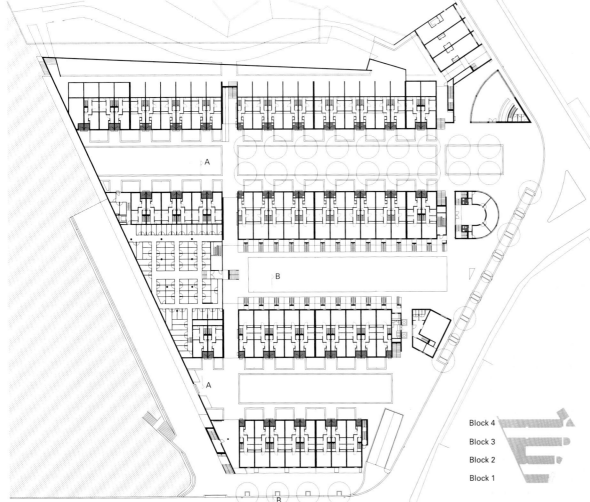

Block 4
Block 3
Block 2
Block 1

Ground-floor plan

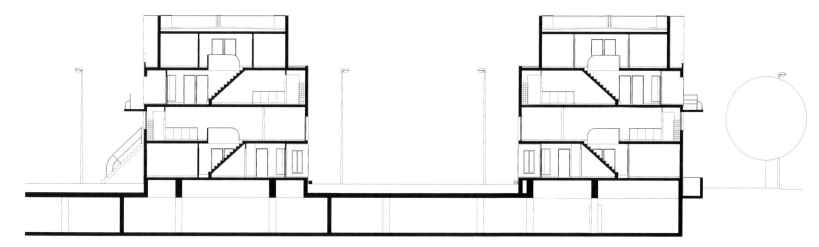

Section A

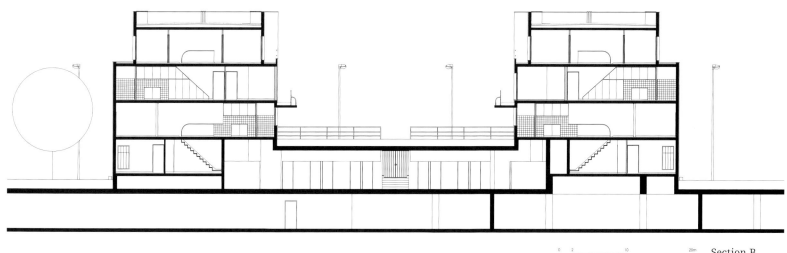

Section B

Opposite above: Courtyard between blocks 3 and 4 of houses. Opposite below: Café at the end of block 3.

Below: Courtyard between blocks 1 and 2 of houses. The staircase provides access to the upper row of flats.

17

Opposite: Passageway from
courtyard through block 4 to
Rua da Boavista.

Below: Typical flat interior,
first floor.

19

View along Rua da Boavista
with block 4 of houses to the left.

Bouça: how much has changed

Carlos Carvalho was born in 1953. He was involved in the Resident's Association of Bouça, from its beginning until 1994. He recently bought a three-room dwelling in one of the new blocks of apartments. He hopes to help recuperate the original spirit of the project to which he devoted his time and his dreams.

What was Bouça before the construction of the residential quarter in 1973?

It was a completely free site, wasteland, which belonged to the Ministry of Justice. There was only one house, which was built in the 1960s by prisoners of the Porto Central Jail, for the jail's warden. By the time that house was completed, the jail had been transferred from the Cordoaria area to the Custóias neighbourhood, so the warden never used it.

How did the idea of building a residential quarter on that land come about?

In 1974, soon after the Revolution, we created the Bouça Resident's Association. We occupied some of the houses that had been previously confiscated by the Ministry of Justice because they overlooked the inside of the jail. We invited families that lived in overcrowded inner-city dwellings to move there, with the intention of vacating the premises when better housing became available. During that same period, SAAL was created by Nuno Portas, the Secretary of State for Housing and Urbanization during the first Provisional Government, with the objective of promoting self-construction.

How did Álvaro Siza come to be involved in this project?

Alexandre Alves Costa, at the time connected with SAAL, was one of the people who encouraged us to occupy these houses precisely because, as he told us, Siza had just 'scribbled a drawing' for that site. So we could barter those houses for the land required to build more suitable homes. Siza's project had been prepared for the Housing Promotion Fund (*Fundo de Formento da Habitação* or FFH) in 1973. It was a risk and we took a chance. At that time, so-called social housing mainly consisted of houses provided by the County Council. It was a model that we rejected, because it didn't respect people; it was against them. In addition to the poor quality of the houses, people were moved away from the neighbourhoods where they had been living. We had a motto: the right to stay in one's place.

What criteria were used to select who would be housed in the new neighbourhood?

We had about 300 families registered and only 56 houses, so there was a need to establish rules. It was a beautiful and magnificent process. It was absolutely exemplary. The decisive criterion was always the extent of need. The economic aspect never prevailed. What did we do? First of all, we surveyed the situation of the 300 people very superficially. Then, we formed inquiry committees for each street. The people of the street chose their own representatives who, in accordance with technical coordinators, would make an estimation of need for each case. The Monte Cativo committee wrote one report, the one for Burgães another, and so on. The final decisions were made by a team composed of the representatives of each street, along with technical personnel (architects and social workers).

How did the process of choosing happen after the second phase of construction?

At this stage, the process had no social aspect to it. The only criterion was to be registered in the Cooperative. As there were few candidates, we had to publicize the fact among the people we knew in order to distribute the remaining houses. As it became known that Siza's social houses were available in Bouça, there was a race, mainly by young people in general and young people connected to architecture in particular, to try to purchase them. Many architects live here. In this second phase, there are people that bought their houses with a view to a future investment and that worries me, because there is no hope at all that they will involve themselves in the development of a social residential quarter. They live in the houses for a while and when the price goes up, they sell them and move away. A similar thing happened with the commercial and social spaces, such as the ATL (an after-school space for children) and the Café. Instead of being used for the aim for which they were designed, they were sold off at a profit.

And how is the relationship between the first set of people and those who have just arrived?

Each set came in a completely different context, with very different motivations and expectations. They are indeed very different people. In the first lot they were working-class people and they tended to be rather old, without any professional or academic background, and not used to well-designed housing. They were confronted with a fantastic space but had difficulties in using it and managing it. The people from the second set are generally young, socially integrated people, without economic difficulties. They came because they liked the area, the way the houses were designed, the project itself… and also because it was a good business investment.

But are there latent conflicts between old residents and those who came recently?

There is no conflict or ill feeling between the ones who came before and the ones who came after. What doesn't exist is a social relationship, because the spaces designed for that purpose were altered, and because the people are not motivated towards community life. But there is a positive aspect that should be emphasized: the arrival of the new residents improved the self-esteem of those who were already there. With the influx of qualified people (for instance, doctors and architects), they thought: after all, they are like us; they live in houses like ours. Well, this raises a sense of self-esteem. It facilitates integration and breaks down social prejudices.

Interview by Nuno Higino, May 2007

Bragança Terraces
Lisbon, Portugal
1992–2004

Bragança Terraces

The Bragança Terraces housing, services and commercial complex occupies a site of about 5,000 square metres, located between Rua António Maria Cardoso and Rua do Alecrim, which appeared as a gap to be filled in an otherwise perfectly consolidated area. We wanted to establish a dialogue with the context, to find the right way to define the project itself, as well as to make an attentive reading of the land, its topography and the footprints left by those who lived on the site and who have given it meaning. These traces go back at least to the beginning of the fourteenth century, the period when the Muralha Fernandina (Ferdinand Wall, named after the king responsible for its construction) enclosing the city was built.

Thus, we constructed a set of three buildings in the area of the site along Rua do Alecrim, all lining the street and each 15.5 metres deep. Their programmatic definition is also similar: the bottom floor or two floors of each building are allocated to trade, and the upper floors are for offices and residential use. At the site's higher area, bordering Rua António Maria Cardoso, two buildings were erected and designated for exclusively residential use. In the original design these buildings made contact with the ground via columns separated by large spans, which were defined so as to preserve the existing ruins of the historic Muralha Fernandina, which substantially increased the value of the site. After consulting with IPPAR (*Instituto Português do Património Arquitectónico*, the organization responsible for the conservation of Portuguese historic architecture) it was agreed to make this area a museum, integrated within the houses' common ground and accessible to the public.

The structure of the building is reinforced concrete, comprising columns and hollow core slabs. The roof surfaces are flat, waterproofed, thermally insulated and covered with vegetation. Along Rua do Alecrim, the building's external finishes are Portuguese limestone up to the top level of offices or commercial spaces, and ceramic tiles on the remaining levels. The buildings along Rua António Maria Cardoso have a base in Portuguese limestone up to the level of the first residential floor, and the remaining wall surfaces are tiled. External windows and doors are in painted timber with double glazing and internal timber shutters for solar protection.

– Álvaro Siza

Above left: Siza's sketches of the facade and cornice detail.
Above right: Sketches showing original scheme to support the blocks on large columns.
Below: Sketches showing possible circulation paths.

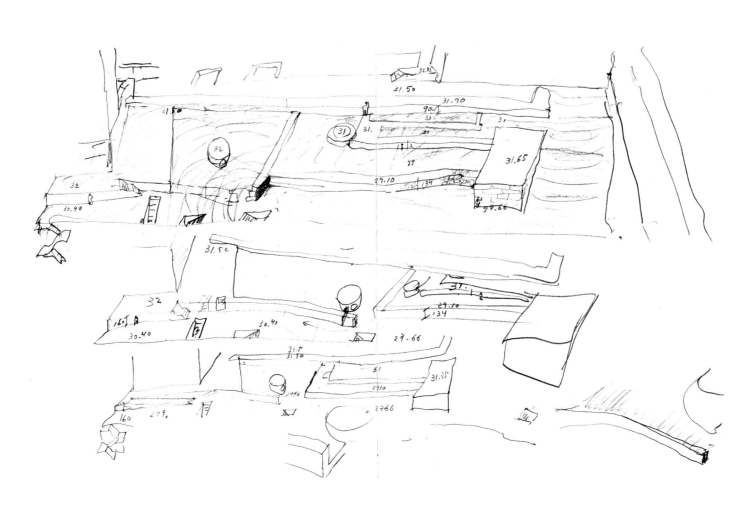

Opposite: Courtyard between
buildings.

Below: Building bordering Rua
do Alecrim. Areas with limestone
facing house commercial space,
and tiled facades indicate
residential floors.

27

Sixth-floor plan

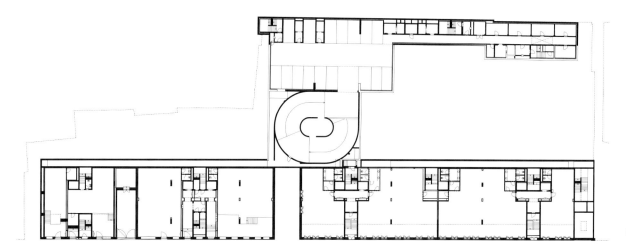

Third-floor plan

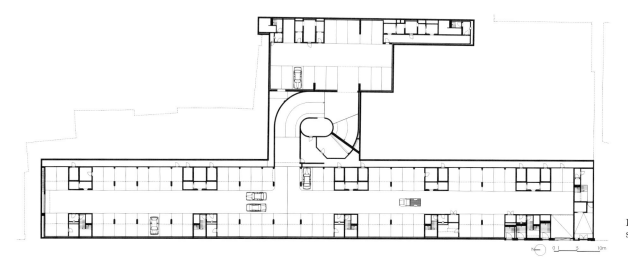

Lower-floor plan,
showing parking

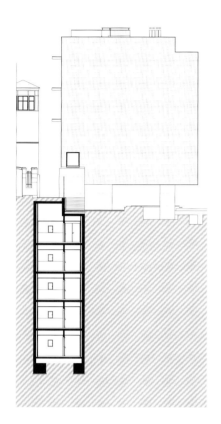

Section A

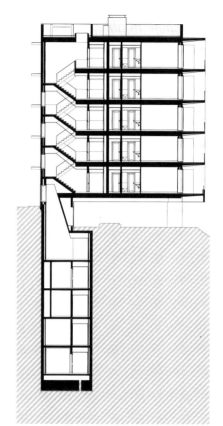

Section B

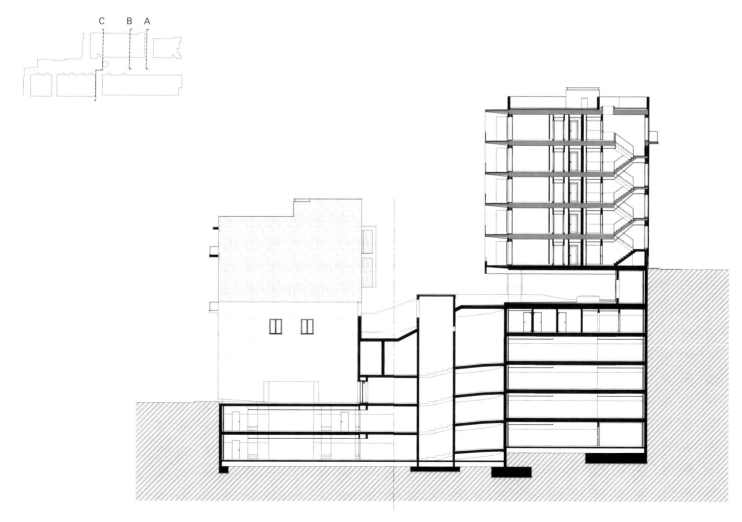

Section C

Opposite: Buildings bordering
Rua do Alecrim.

Below: Buildings bordering Rua
do Alecrim, seen from building
bordering Rua António Maria
Cardoso.

31

The options

The Bragança Terraces project was started during the vital stages of the recovery of Chiado (a Lisbon neighbourhood largely restored by Siza after a huge fire destroyed a number of structures in 1988). The then client and landowner for Bragança Terraces had not been able to finalize or agree on anything for decades. The process was dragging along, without anyone showing the courage to make any decision at all. In large part, this was because there were (and still are) ruins on the site that had to be protected. It was a enormous hole that remained open for over 40 years. In 1992, the desires of the disparate parties were finally resolved and the process began. The landowner attained his objective of selling the land, and Siza came on as the architect for the site. During Siza's work on the Chiado recovery, the design process had raised many questions: what to recover, what to make anew, what breaks should be made with what remained and with what was burnt down? Although the recovery of Chiado presented difficulties, the reconstruction option allowed the use of known models, maintaining rigour, adapting uses and creating new urban spaces and routes. The process was slow and never complete. In Bragança Terraces, the questions were different. There had been no fire, the building had been demolished, there were few records, and we had to preserve the ruins of Muralha Fernandina and Palácio dos Duques de Bragança (Ducal Palace of Bragança). On the terraces the need was to be even more precise, more delicate and complex, and with other parameters: to make anew, within an urban fabric that was fixed but also needed consolidation. Once again, doubts emerged: a clean break or mimesis? Siza's decision was to interpret and follow history. The history of the city, of that specific block, of the Tejo river, of the luxury apartments that came to replace the old ones, which had themselves once been luxurious before they had become delapidated and divided into smaller spaces. Their materials are always timeless, always current, worn-out but of great beauty. Now when I go up or down Rua do Alecrim, the reflections, the connections and proportions tell me that something has changed in the course of a prolonged contemporariness and that something has extended the city without denying it or even adulterating it. There is so much other land to tear, to break, to try out new ideas and new suggestions in the natural progression of aesthetics. It is a pity that the ruins didn't end up being part of the public realm, as the design had envisaged.

– Carlos Castanheira

The terraces, to the left, facing a fragment of the Muralha Fernandina (Ferdinand Wall).

Insel-Hombroich Foundation
Museum of Architecture
Hombrich, Germany
1995–2008

Insel-Hombroich Foundation Museum of Architecture

This project is one of the examples of Siza's perseverance. Before it became a museum project, in 1995 this was to be an institute of biophysics. Various ideas and opportunities shaped the brief over the 13 years that this project took to materialize. Patiently, the architect continued responding to these successive changes, while maintaining his fundamental objective, that of building. And he succeeded.

The site had been occupied by an old military camp that was decommissioned, making it possible for it to be acquired by the Insel-Hombroich Foundation, which invited various architects to design different kinds of cultural facilities for the small river island. The overall project is essentially a landscape project because the design manipulates what a visitor sees on arrival, during the visit, while staying and on departing.

Access is by means of an excavated ditch. Approaching the building on its southern side, the first things we see are the roofs. Following a natural path, we arrive at a patio walled on two sides, which limits our views to the north.We have arrived at the museum. We enter via the western facade. The entrance is well defined, leaving no one in doubt of the correct path. The floor inside is slightly raised from the outside level. From the foyer we gain access to a reception and administrative area. To the south are the women's lavatories. Continuing on to the north, there is a sequence of three rooms dedicated to the architects who worked for the foundation, including Frei Otto, Álvaro Siza and Raimund Abraham. Light enters these rooms through the doors that open on to the patio which is formed by the main building. Moving east along a corridor that will also act as an exhibition space, we find, halfway along, the temporary exhibition room. Looking to the north and the south one can see the landscape and make out Düsseldorf's skyline, perfectly framed and contained, as defined by the architect, as he intended for us to see them. Further along the corridor on its internal angle, we find the men's lavatories, a small kitchen and support spaces. Further ahead and already moving north, we reach the small auditorium, which accommodates about 40 people. This space is lowered so as to create an amphitheatre, without altering the height of the ceilings or the roofs. A twisting in the auditorium's west facade – the only non-orthogonal element in the building – allows in light and ventilation, and also provides an emergency exit. Outside, a terrace is not only a place to be but also serves as a circulation area between the exhibition spaces and the auditorium. Following on, we arrive at three more spaces allocated to architects, the first being dedicated to the work of Erwin Heerich.

A photographic archive is housed in the volume attached to the museum building by the long wall that separates the patio from the landscape. It consists of an entrance, a circulation area, two small technical areas and two archive spaces. The archives have openings that allow in natural light from the north and access to an almost-private patio. Inside, the floors are in oak and the ceilings are constructed of oak timber beams and sheeting. The walls are plastered and white. In the lavatories, the floor and part of the walls are finished in Moleanos limestone.

Outside, the almost total horizontality of the building, which is broken only by the fenestration, is accentuated by the re-use of bricks salvaged from the demolition of the original buildings. The parallel pattern emphasizes the long planes of the building, blurring the walls that define the interior space and those that define the exterior space. Despite this, the building has a very intimate quality.

The Insel-Hombroich Foundation Museum of Architecture is one of those small buildings that due to its calm, its restraint and its appropriate use of materials seems almost banal. But exploring more closely, we appreciate the richness of the spaces, the mastery of the planning and the tranquillity that it transmits. We appreciate that a great work of architecture can actually be small in size. We appreciate too, that perseverance is also an art.

– Carlos Castanheira

Sketches showing the building in the landscape and the gallery sequence.

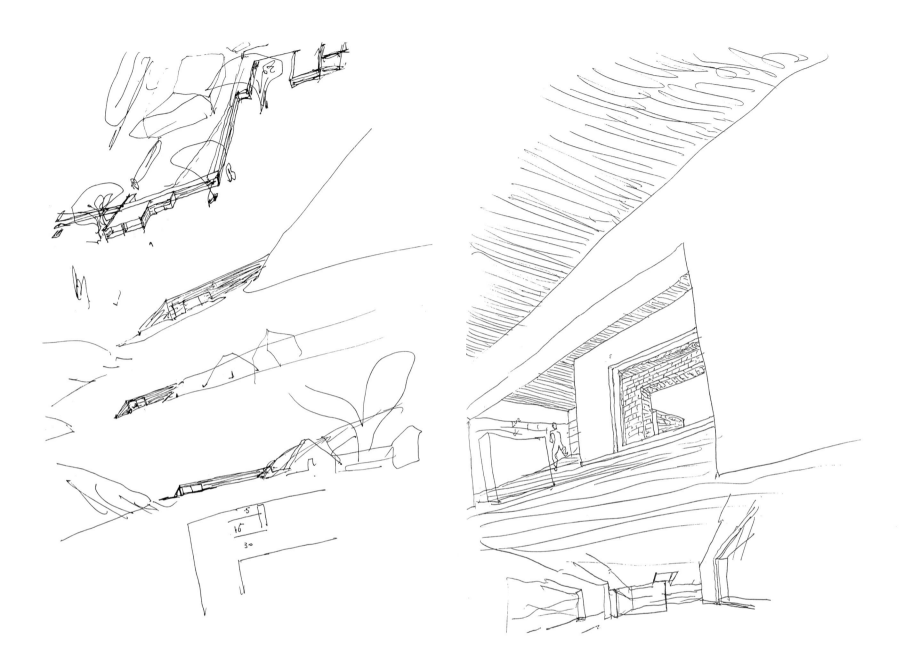

View of the museum from the west.

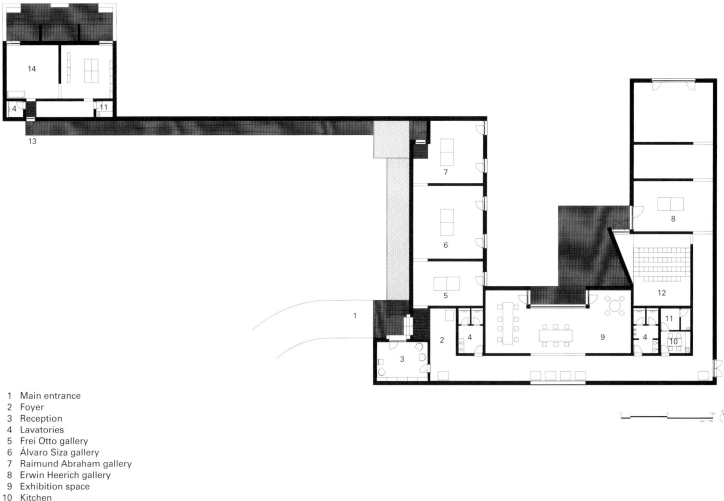

1   Main entrance
2   Foyer
3   Reception
4   Lavatories
5   Frei Otto gallery
6   Álvaro Siza gallery
7   Raimund Abraham gallery
8   Erwin Heerich gallery
9   Exhibition space
10 Kitchen
11 Technical area
12 Auditorium
13 Photo archive entrance
14 Photo archive

Ground-floor plan

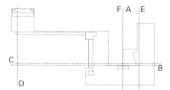

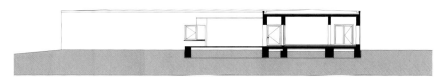

Section A

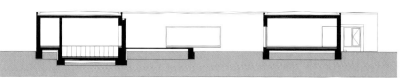

Section B

Section C

Section D

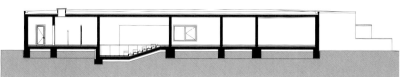

Section E

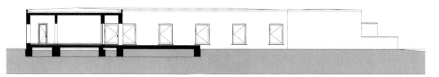

Section F

Opposite: View of the museum from the south.

Below: The large window faces south, bringing light into the museum and allowing views on to the surrounding landscape.

43

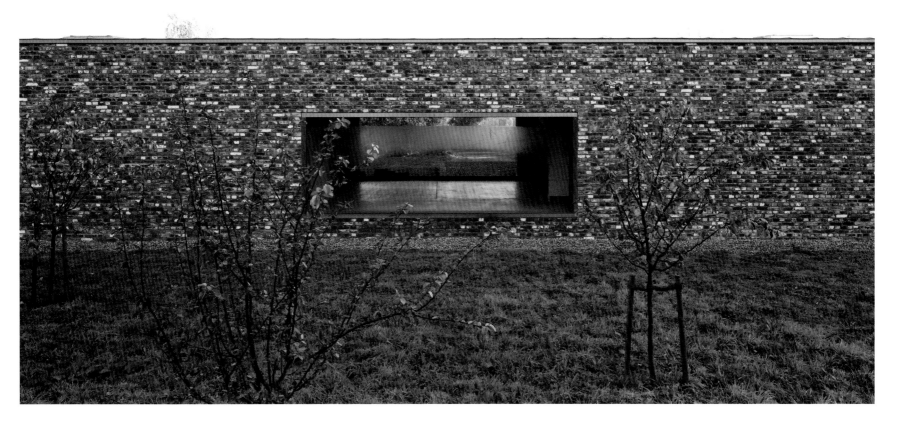

Above: The main entrance to the museum.

Opposite: View into the foyer and the exhibition space from the north.

Insel-Hombroich Foundation
Museum of Architecture

Below: Auditorium seen from the
entrance.

Opposite: Auditorium (above)
and view through the galleries
(below).

São Bento Underground Station
Porto, Portugal
1997–2005

Such a station

The new Porto underground, a project won in competition by the architect Eduardo Souto de Moura, is a significant undertaking for the city. It was always going to be a controversial piece of work. After being awarded the project, Souto de Moura established a set of rules for other architects, who were allocated work in different areas. He coordinated. The design of the São Bento underground station was entrusted to Siza, with the same rules and directions as the other stations. I am certain that Siza's reaction must have been: *isto não é pêra doce*! (This is not a sweet pear!), as he is known to often exclaim. São Bento is the most central station in the city, but not, however, the main one: such glory goes to the Trindade station. But São Bento is definitely the most complex, determined by the most constraints. Access points are all at different levels: from Rua 31 de Janeiro on the north side, via Rua do Loureiro and through the side entrance of the old São Bento station to the south, and from Praça de Almeida Garrett and Rua das Flores to the west. The entrances to the north give access to what we call the high mezzanine, and those to the south lead to the low mezzanine. These mezzanines organize routes, distribute passengers and overcome complex differences in level. At the lower level, the mezzanine facilitates access to trains and platforms, where the waiting time is generally short. Scant space between buildings and the limitations imposed by the necessary continuity of the trainline generated this complex work of design and engineering, which also resulted in a redesign of the urban space it occupies. The low mezzanine is defined by two rows of columns that are suspended from the upper structure of the roof (which doubles as pavement on the exterior). These columns support, in tension, the paving stone of the platform canopy. With this upside-down structure, all spaces gain diversity. Also here, as usual, design and structural calculation work together. The roofs, which are not false but are suspended, create form, join platforms, and generate new perspectives.
The finishing materials and fixtures are the same throughout the whole Porto underground network. In this station, however, they acquire a different soul from the colour and the elegant graffito line, which invites a search, as if playing a game or a joke. As always, the irony is disconcerting, even disturbing. São Bento will be happy to have such a station. I am. And surely many other people are as well.

– Carlos Castanheira

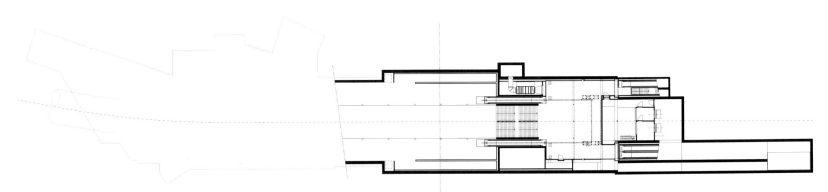

High mezzanine floor plan

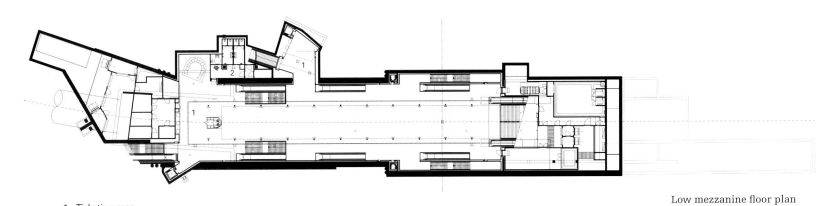

Low mezzanine floor plan

1 Ticketing area
2 Lavatories
3 Platform

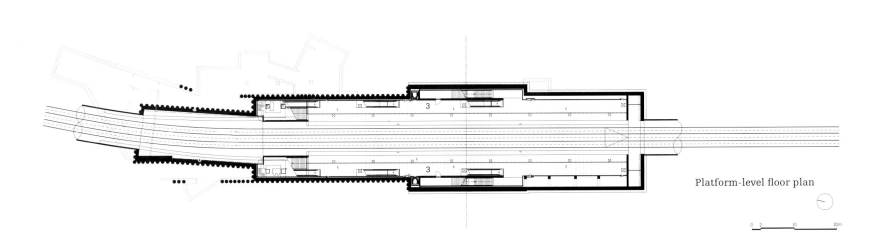

Platform-level floor plan

0 2   10   20m

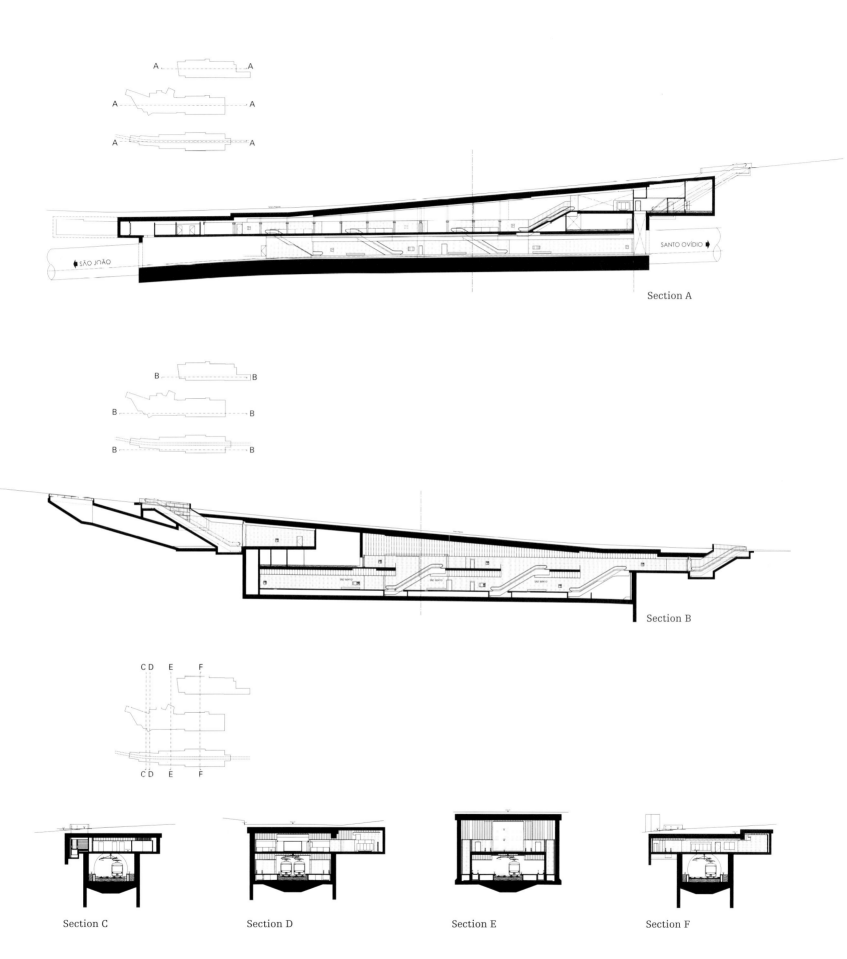

Section A

Section B

Section C   Section D   Section E   Section F

Adventurous lines

An underground station is a place of passage (and one undertaken at speed), not a place of permanence. At the boarding platform there may be a couple of minutes' wait, but access routes to that point are traversed at a fast pace, and in this station the only thing that the eyes can catch along the way – although they have no time to settle on them – are flying images.

The sketched lines over the tiling are essentially self-referential. They live to be sketches; they show themselves and they hide themselves, almost ignoring any figurative preoccupation or requirement. The figurative references are vague, suggesting at times more or less familiar images. The line, which in a drawing generally disappears to give way to the figure, here, presents and exposes itself as such.

On the other hand, the background against which this line operates is not homogeneous: it is formed by a squared web of soft and varied tones of colour. The lines tearing through those tiles are therefore cut lines, which slice and discontinue themselves. There are lines that take risks and dare to cross border after border. They are transgressive lines, a quality easily missed by the quick glance of those who pass by and overlook the analytical test and visual dissection. The usual authority of vision, dizzy and weakened by the madness of rush hour, shuts its eyes when passing through the effects of those adventurous lines.

But there are also 'good' lines that rescind themselves to give way to the figure. Small shapes are arranged in the space to which they were assigned, within the squareness of the tiles. Those do not risk the crossing of the border. Maybe this is because they are fearful of the power of a less-hurried look, with time to stop and wait for the next composition.

– Nuno Higino

Above: Low mezzanine level. Siza's sketches are reproduced as black lines on the coloured tile walls throughout the station. Below: Platform level.

Zaida Building, Patio House
Granada, Spain
1993–2006

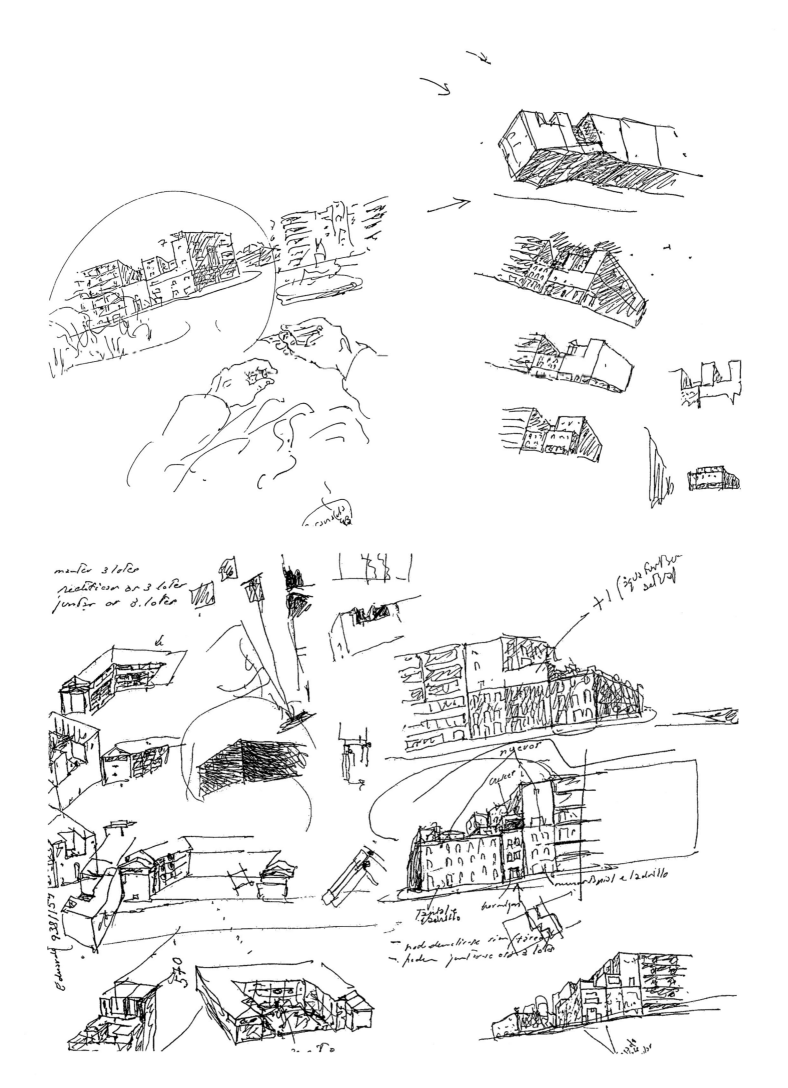

Zaida Building, Patio House

This building defines the southern end of a square in Granada, known as Fuente de las Batallas. The project appropriated three different lots, all of which had previously been built on. The old Hotel Zaida, a four-storey building, was situated on one lot; a recently constructed building, also a four-storey structure, was located on the second; and on the third site, with access from Carrera de Genil, was an old house of certain architectural merit, built around two patios in a typology common to the old urban fabric of Granada. Since the end of the nineteenth century the square has suffered many transformations, both architecturally and in terms of town-planning, which led to the complete disappearance of the original urban grain. Since the river Darro was channelled in 1884, the square has been slowly gaining importance and today is more or less the centre of the city.

The older existing building, the house with the two-patio arrangement, was maintained, although the facade was modified in order to be integrated into the scheme. The buildings on the other plots were demolished to make way for a new, six-storey volume, which maintains the same height as the surrounding area, and has a seven-storey end-piece facing the square.

This volumetric arrangement gives a new face to Fuente de las Batallas, with a scale more appropriate to that of the surrounding edifices. It also acts as a bookend to the city block that it completes. It is for this reason that the facade facing the square contains the highest point of the building, standing about 21 metres over the street, visually approximating the height of the closest building, which is situated between Calle Puente de Castañeda and the square itself.

At the same time, where it connects with the rest of the existing building line, the proposed building maintains their height: 6 storeys, 19 metres. The broken form of the western facade responds to the memory of the route of the Darro river. Above the second floor, on the facade overlooking Carrera de Genil, the building opens up into a U-shape to allow better views of the Alhambra. It is built in reinforced concrete, with stone facing up to the top of the first floor and finished above in white-painted render.

– Álvaro Siza

Fuente de las Batallas.

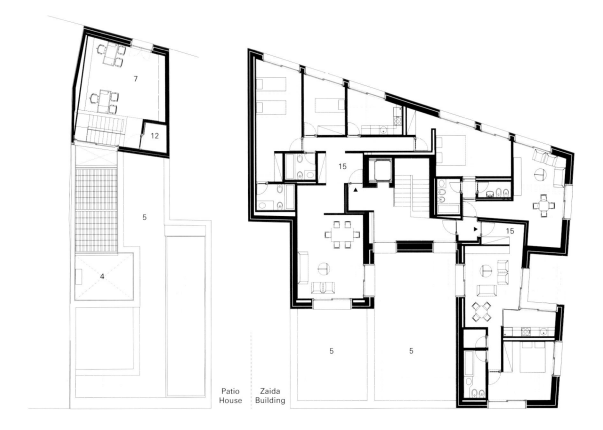

Patio House Zaida Building

Fifth-floor plan

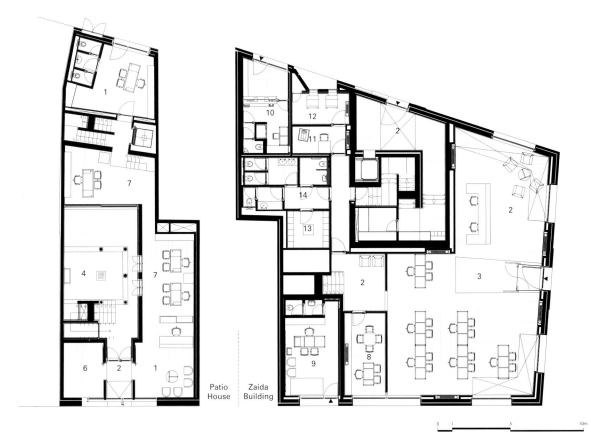

Patio House Zaida Building

1   Reception
2   Lobby
3   Public hall
4   Patio
5   Terrace
6   Exhibition space
7   Office
8   Manager's office
9   Real estate agency
10 State lottery office
11 Treasury
12 Equipment room
13 Storage
14 Lavatory
15 Flat

Ground-floor plan

0   1   5   10m

Patio House   Zaida Building

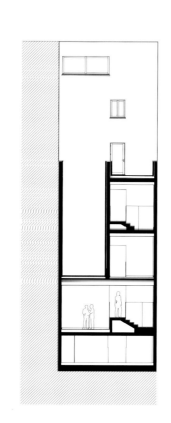

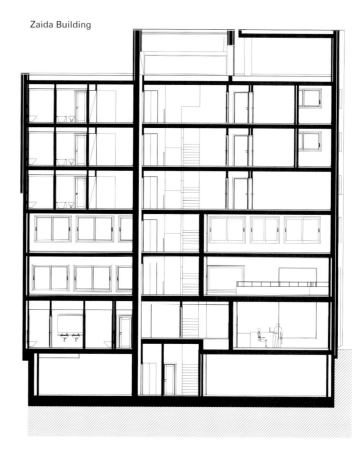

Section A

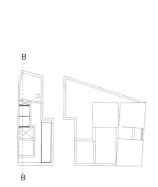

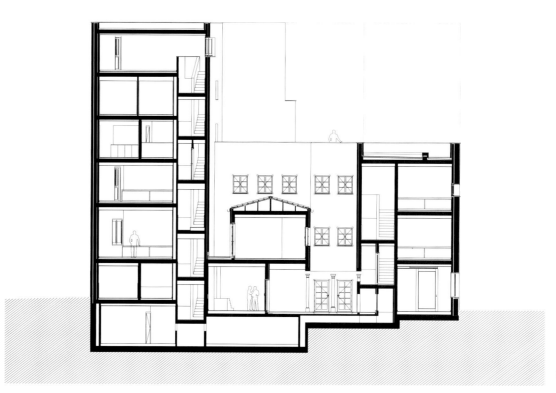

Section B

Opposite: Southern patio, from
the ground floor (above) and
seen from the third floor (below).

Below: Looking north from the
third floor.

71

From the Alhambra you can see Sierra Nevada

In Granada there is a square. In Granada there is the Alhambra. In Granada there is *tablado*, the place where *flamenco* is danced. In Granada there are patios and patio houses. In Granada there are Andalucian men and women: *Granadinas*. In Granada there is the Sierra Nevada. In Granada there is Granada and now, in its architecture, there is Álvaro Siza.

In a very central square, a building has sprung up. It is actually two buildings in one, like a small city, which contains variety in unity. One building within the building, with a variety of functions, is hierarchical, tidy, ordered. These functions are arranged in a traditional manner: commercial at ground level; offices, called *oficinas* here, in the middle levels; and at the top, in a privileged position, the residential units. The other is a patio house. There are many such houses here but they remain invisible, because they are arranged around a patio that by definition is internal: cool, private, a typology of Arabian origin. The interior of the house was maintained, this typology kept, but the facade was remodelled because it lacked both constructive and architectural quality. Not all that existed before and was preserved has quality. We have to stand up and conquer the fear that everything that is built now is of a lesser quality than that which is old. Although unfortunately – and unflatteringly for us architects – this is true more often than not.

The new Zaida Building, a name inherited from the building that existed on the site and is now demolished, faces both the square and the city, as seen from the different perspectives of the *calles del casco antiguo*. It becomes the conclusion, the beginning, and the face of this hinged space. In its morphology and volumetric arrangement we can discern the designer's concern to integrate, into both the constructed mass of the city and the open space, the void that is always full of life, varied and rhythmic, as in a *tablado*, deeply Andalucian. There is much that overflows from within: life that happens indoors becomes connected with the outside, passing people come and go. The inhabitants of this building are cohabitating with the city. And then there is the Alhambra, always present, always marking its location: that was its purpose. But from the Alhambra, one can also look over the city and the square, under the Sierra Nevada.

– Carlos Castanheira

The Sierra Nevada seen from
Fuente de las Batallas.

Iberê Camargo Foundation Museum
Porto Alegre, Brazil
1998–2008

Iberê Camargo Foundation Museum

The main purpose of this building is to house the archive and exhibit the work of Iberê Camargo, a well-known Brazilian painter. In addition to exhibition space, the complex includes artists' workshops, a small auditorium, a book and video library, a bookstore, a café, administrative offices and storage space. The enthusiasm and support of the artist's widow was essential to the project, and a group of sponsors guaranteed viability of the museum, which is run by the Iberê Camargo Foundation.

The Porto Alegre city government offered the land for the building, a former stone quarry with very little vegetative cover. The site is relatively small and narrow, bordered on the north by the busy Avenida Padre Cacique and on the south by a very steep cliff that rises from 5 to 24 metres. The exquisite view stretches over the Guaíba river, one of those South American rivers so wide that they appear to be sea.

The main difficulty we faced was harmonizing the museum's needs with such a narrow plot of land. We also had to resolve the problem that there was no land available for parking, since the basement was to be used for archive storage and the small auditorium. The solution was to build the car-park above the avenue, and to develop the museum as a vertical construction. The building's base is a long platform, 0.6 metres above the level of the avenue and accessible from the avenue walkway by a ramp. The artists' workshops, used for teaching and apprenticeship, are located in an annexe at one end of this platform. At the other, storage, administrative space and the auditorium are housed underneath the platform, and above, the principal volume is carved out from the cliff and occupies its naturally concave space. This four-floor volume is delimited by straight walls on the south and west, and by an undulating wall on the north and east. The undulating wall, which mirrors the shape of the slope against which it is built, rises the entire height of the building and defines one edge of a central atrium. The other side of the atrium consists of an L-shape, which on the ground floor (the level of the platform) contains the reception, cloak-room, and bookstore. On the three floors above, this space is used for the exhibition galleries, which are three rooms of varying dimensions on each floor.

Permanent and temporary exhibition spaces are not differentiated, giving the museum, which frequently assembles temporary shows from its collection, the necessary level of flexibility. The rooms of all the floors can be opened on to the atrium space, which receives natural light from a skylight and from exterior openings on the undulating wall. The exhibition rooms can also be closed off with movable 4-metre-high panels, which are short enough to allow in natural light from the atrium between the top of the panels and the ceiling. The rooms of the top floor also receive natural light from skylights made from double-paned glass, which is accessible for cleaning and maintenance.

The vertical access points (two lifts and two sets of stairs), are situated at each end of the sequence of exhibition galleries. A continuous walkway leading up and down through the sequence is also achieved via ramps that run partially along the edge of the internal atrium and partially as paths that cantilever off the exterior of the building, forming three separate loops that each detach from and then re-join the main volume. This creates small, closed galleries surrounding the volume of the building, with skylights and small openings on to the beautiful landscape.

– Álvaro Siza

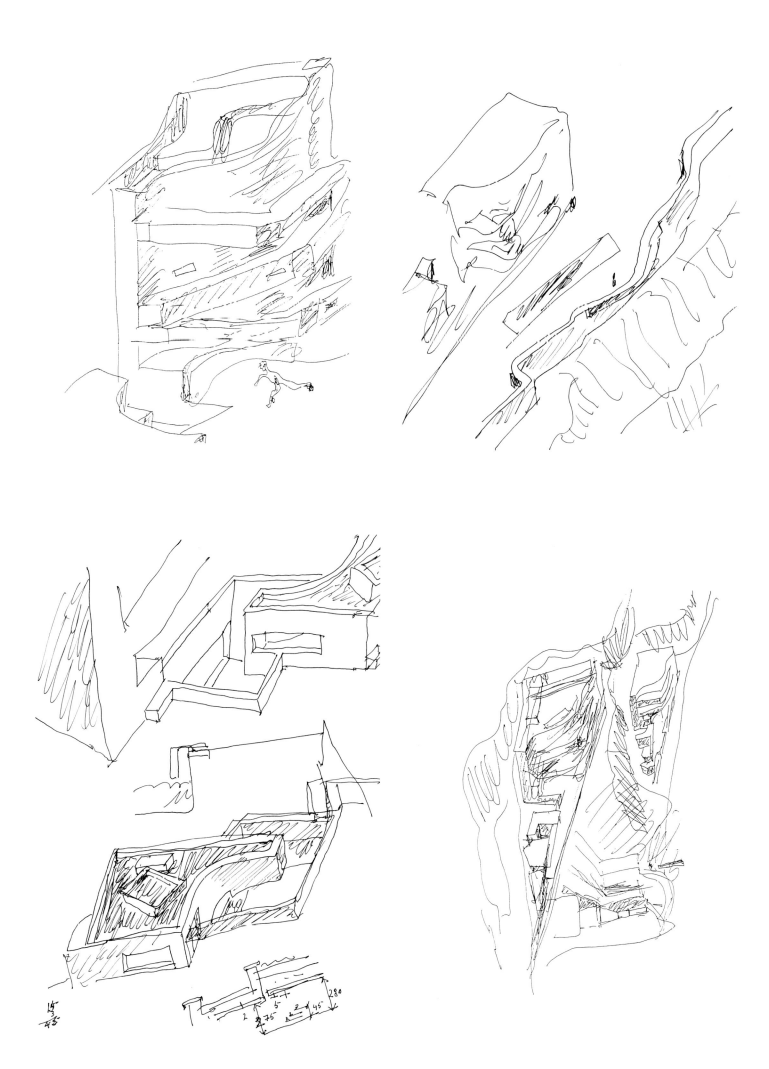

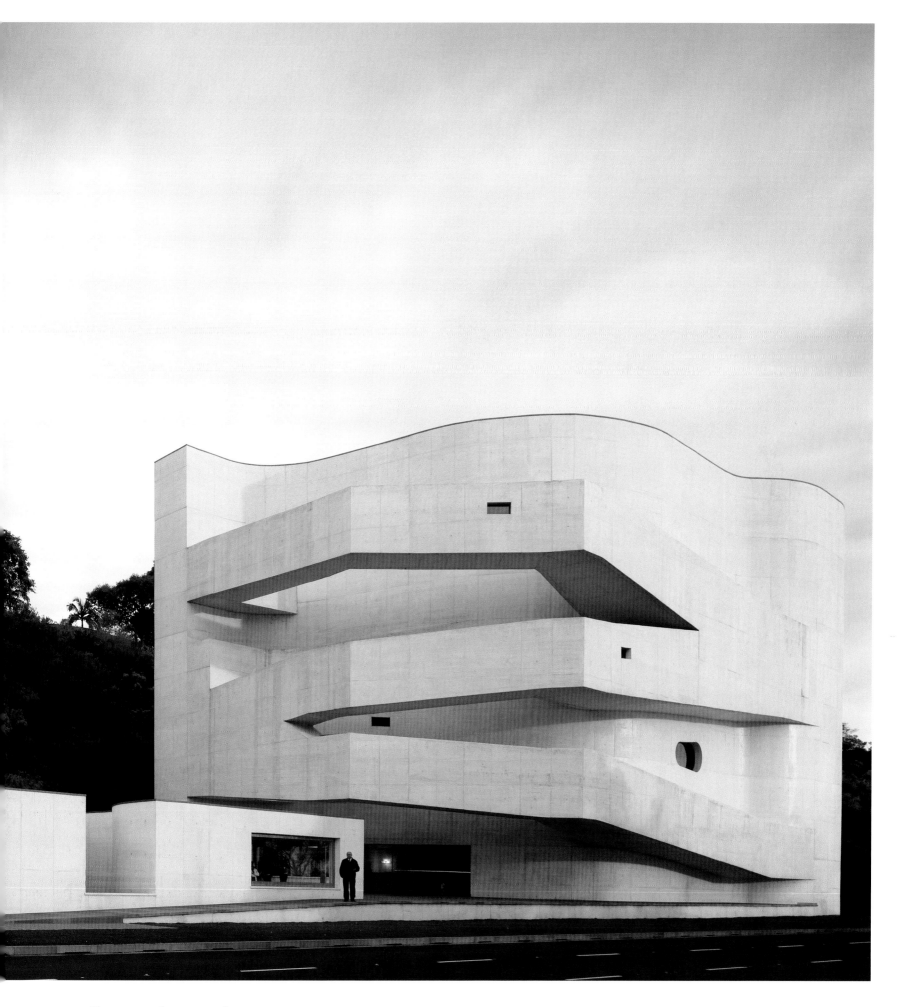

Museum seen from across the
highway. Artist's workshops are
located in the low buildings to
the left.

Opposite: View towards main
entrance from the northeast.

Below: Detail of thick circulation
wall separating the exterior
courtyard from the interior
atrium.

81

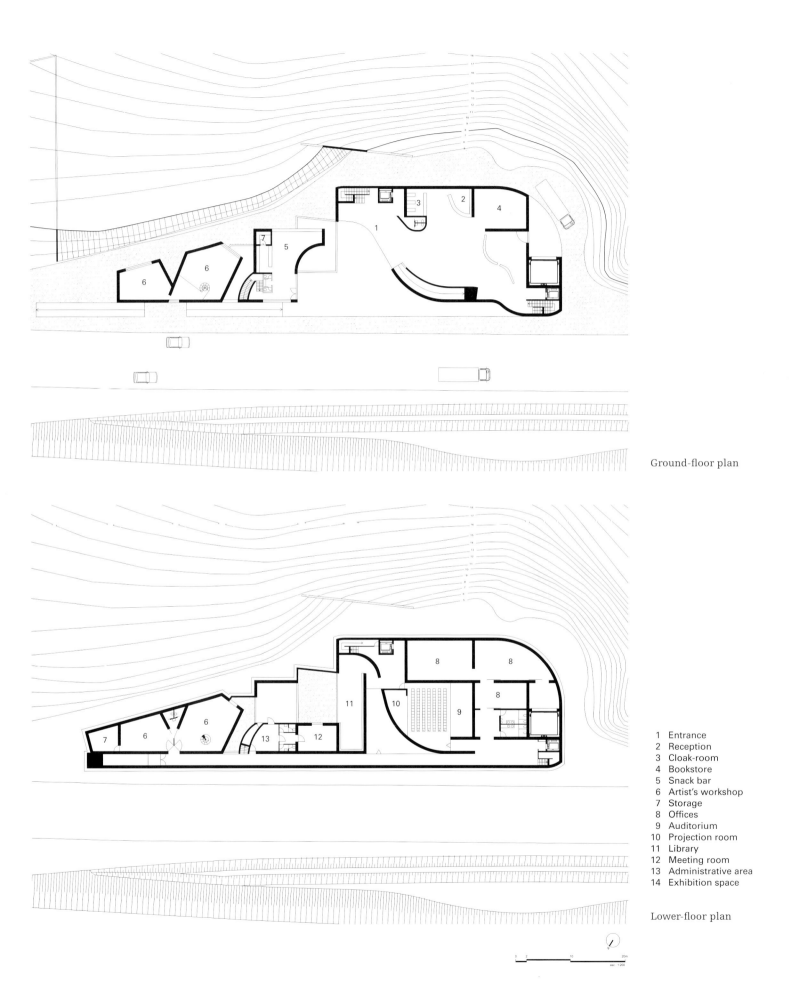

Ground-floor plan

Lower-floor plan

1 Entrance
2 Reception
3 Cloak-room
4 Bookstore
5 Snack bar
6 Artist's workshop
7 Storage
8 Offices
9 Auditorium
10 Projection room
11 Library
12 Meeting room
13 Administrative area
14 Exhibition space

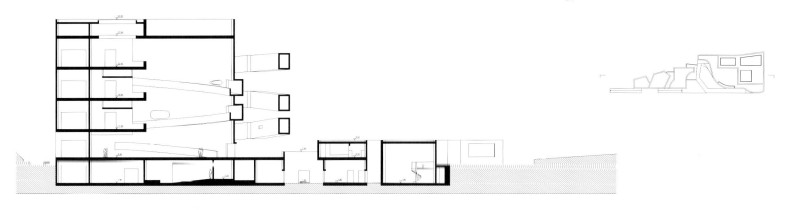

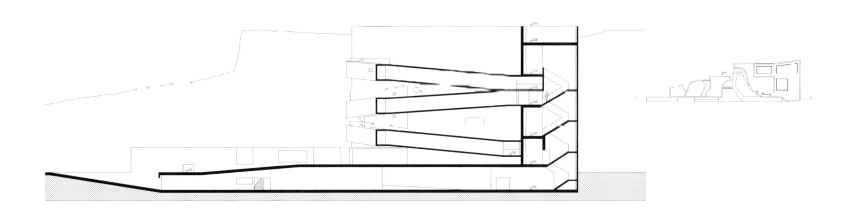

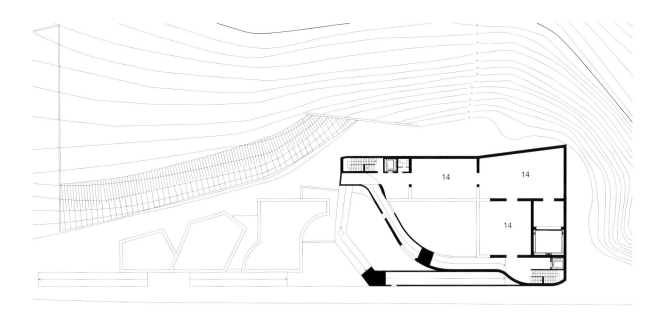

Third-floor plan

Atrium interior with circulation ramp.

Centre for 'Camilian' Studies
Vila Nova de Famalicão, Portugal
1998–2005

Centre for 'Camilian' Studies

The Cultural Centre of Camilo Castelo Branco is a complex that includes the Centre for 'Camilian' Studies, as well as the house of Camilo Castelo Branco (1825–90) and the house of his son, Nuno. Branco, perhaps the most prolific Portuguese writer, lived here for 26 years. As Nuno's house, which has been transformed into a house for guests, was contiguous with both Branco's original house (now a museum) and the new centre, it was decided to keep one access point for the whole complex. Through the original house, a renovated garden configuration gives access to the other two structures. This entry route leads to a patio flanked by three volumes, housing the reading room, the exhibition room, and the hallway and reception area. These volumes, which are never all visible at the same time, are surrounded by the garden, re-built walls and vine pergolas.
The great hallway is the access point for all the different components of the centre, both public areas and internal service areas. This includes the exhibition space, the auditorium, the coffee shop and the administrative areas. The exhibition space, which is lit both naturally and artificially, is subdivided into three areas of different dimensions and can also be accessed directly from the patio. The service areas and the archive are located at the lower level, which, due to the slope of the site, has direct access to the street surrounding the property.
The centre as a whole has an area of 2,315 square metres and is articulated around three landscaped patios, so as to achieve a good distribution of natural light and the correct scale in relation to the dimensions and residential character of the context.

– Álvaro Siza

Above: Sketch studying building form and entry sequence.
Below: Sketch of interior space.

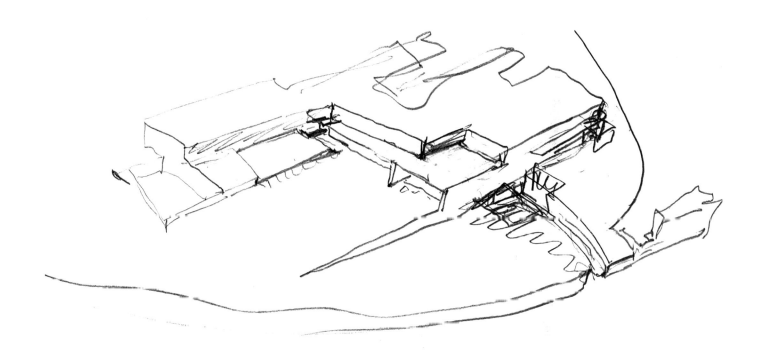

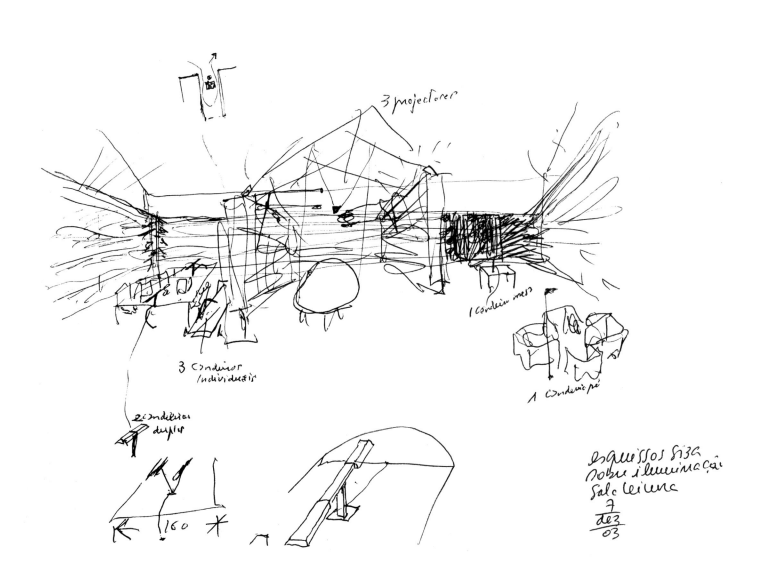

3 projectores

1 Condeium mess

3 Condeias
Individuais

1 Condeu pé

2 candeias
dupler

160

esquissos Siza
sobre iluminação
Sala leitura
7
dez
03

Opposite: View of the centre
from the southwest (above)
and from the south (below).

Below: Aerial view of the Centre.
Camilo Branco's house is
situated at the lower centre
of the photograph.

99

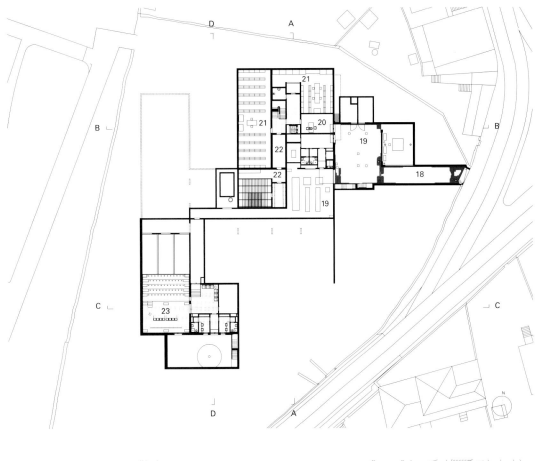

First-floor plan

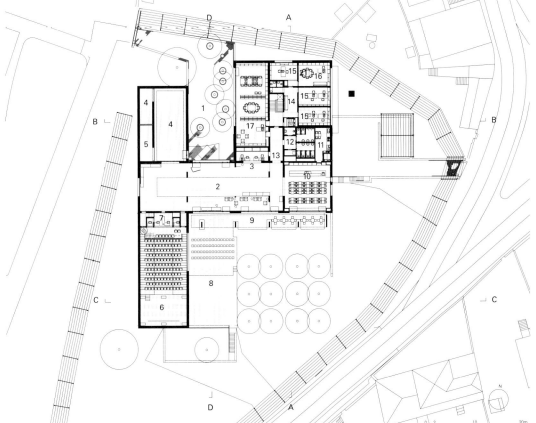

1 Main entrance
2 Public lobby
3 Information
4 Exhibition space
5 Storage
6 Auditorium
7 Projection room
8 Exterior auditorium
9 Patio
10 Cafeteria
11 Kitchen
12 Lavatories
13 Service lobby
14 Office lobby
15 Administrative offices
16 Director's office
17 Reading room
18 Service entrance
19 Service area
20 Book deposit lobby
21 Book deposit
22 Rare book deposit
23 Auditorium service area

Ground-floor plan

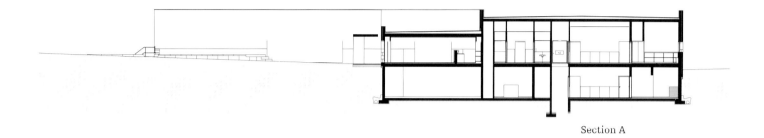

Section A

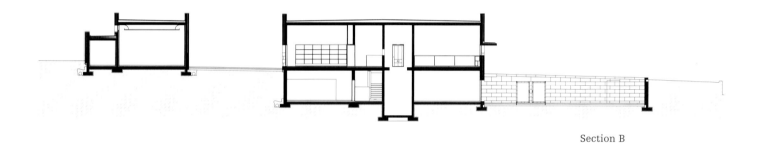

Section B

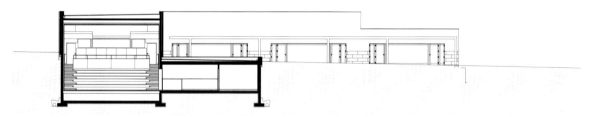

Section C

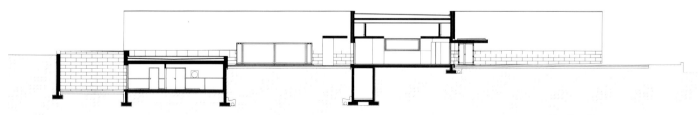

Section D

0 1   5   10m

Below: Sunken courtyard at
night. Camilo Branco's house
is across the street.

Opposite above: Shaded
overhang on entry patio.
Opposite below: Lobby with
view to the entry patio.

The ghost who lives on the other side of the street

Camilo Castelo Branco was born in Lisbon in 1825. He came to live in the house in Seide-São Miguel (now part of Vila Nova de Famalicão) in 1864, where he spent the last 26 years of his tempestuous life. He lived there with Ana Plácido, the wife of a Porto businessman, with whom he had an adulterous affair, for which they were both imprisoned. After Ana's husband died, they settled in Seide, and Camilo wrote prolifically in order to support his family until, facing illness and blindness, he committed suicide in 1890. The house, although carefully kept, had become insufficient for the requirements of the preservation of the writer's memory. It was therefore decided to construct a new building opposite the existing one, across a roadway, to house the Centre for 'Camilian' Studies.

Visitors enter via a modest iron gate and are led around the building in a clockwise manner, following a pathway beneath a vine pergola. After two 90-degree turns, the path ends in a patio where two beech trees, set a little apart, and three or four almond trees that stand closer together, look over and protect the reading room. The trees also break up the coolness of the stone paving. Through the main door is a generous hallway from which circulation to different parts of the centre is organized. Here, the landscape opens up to a 180-degree panorama and a new perspective is presented, over the apple tree and rhododendron garden and across the road, back to Camilo's house. Now we see, facing each other, the two buildings dedicated to preserving and keeping alive the memory of Camilo. Each building is reflected in the other and mirrors the its counterpart's expressions, conjuring up multiple images, memories, possibilities, struggles and expectations. An inheritance is not a passive repository, locked up in a safe to keep it from decay, dissemination and loss. An inheritance should be an active (and as such, necessarily selective) affirmation of a legacy by its inheritors, although even their responsibility and faithfulness cannot guard against infidelity and waywardness.

The aim of the Centre for 'Camilian' Studies is to enrich the memory of Camilo and to project the writer's work, through reading and re-reading, interpretation and re-interpretation. The centre faces Camilo's own house, opens itself to it, as if sneaking a view of the ghosts that inhabit it or maybe negotiating with them (because ghosts cannot be governed, directed or subjugated – but are disposed to doing business). The inheritance is a responsibility that the centre tries to articulate through a memory that is open to its ghosts; just as the new building opens itself from within to the old mansion, where Camilo, exhausted from so much fighting, settled accounts with his own ghosts.

– Nuno Higino

Gallery space with an exhibition
on Camilo Branco.

Multipurpose Pavilion
Gondomar, Portugal
2001–2007

Multipurpose Pavilion

The site for this pavilion occupies a total area of 29,200 square metres and is located to the northeast of an exit off the Gondomar motorway. In addition to the building itself, 5,500 square metres of the plot was allocated to a car-park accommodating 260 vehicles and, southeast of the motorway, there is parking for another 650 cars, occupying almost 12,900 square metres.

The complex comprises three parts: a large elliptical room, a volume for support services, and another small volume for storage and technical areas. These three pieces are arranged so as to create an area to the southeast of the main volume of about 520 square metres, covered by a thin, curvilinear shell of concrete. This protected area includes the entry to the pavilion for both the public and the administrative staff. To the northeast a loading bay with access restricted to building staff is located between the large ellipse and the small storage volume. The entrance for athletes, guests, journalists and other VIPs is located on the southwest side of the building.

The elliptical volume is defined by two axes, which are 104.4 and 84 metres long. Its perimeter, which varies in height from 15.5 to 21.4 metres, is a reinforced-concrete double wall covered with a steel trellis. The pavilion required numerous transition spaces, such as entrances for the public and performers, loading and unloading access points, and emergency exits, which are located at ground-floor level, in the zone between the two halves of the double wall. This zone, which rises the entire height of the building, also houses all the services that need to be accessed from the interior. On the ground floor, this includes a security point and a first-aid room. As it rises to the first and second floors, this interstitial zone contains toilet facilities and VIP spaces, as well as ducts, service routes and areas for technical equipment. At the emergency exits, which are placed diagonally across from each other, the interior wall is curved towards the exterior so that the exits are enlarged and clearly demarcated from within the building.

The central arena of the hall measures 54 x 32 metres, which can contain the standard international size courts for handball (20 x 40 metres), ice hockey (22 x 44 metres), basketball (15 x 28 metres), volleyball (9 x 18 metres), as well as gymnastics and other sports that require smaller playing areas. This sporting zone as a whole allows the simultaneous use for training purposes of two basketball courts and one volleyball court, or three basketball courts.

Along the four sides of this sporting zone rise four upright seating stands. One of these is entirely retractable, in order to enable large performances, and three of the sixteen rows of each of the other three stands can also be taken out. The maximum seating capacities are 3,544 for sporting events and 6,500 for performances. The space under the fixed seating section is partially usable, and forms one element of a space that is available for different activities, such as exhibitions, fairs and meetings.

– Álvaro Siza

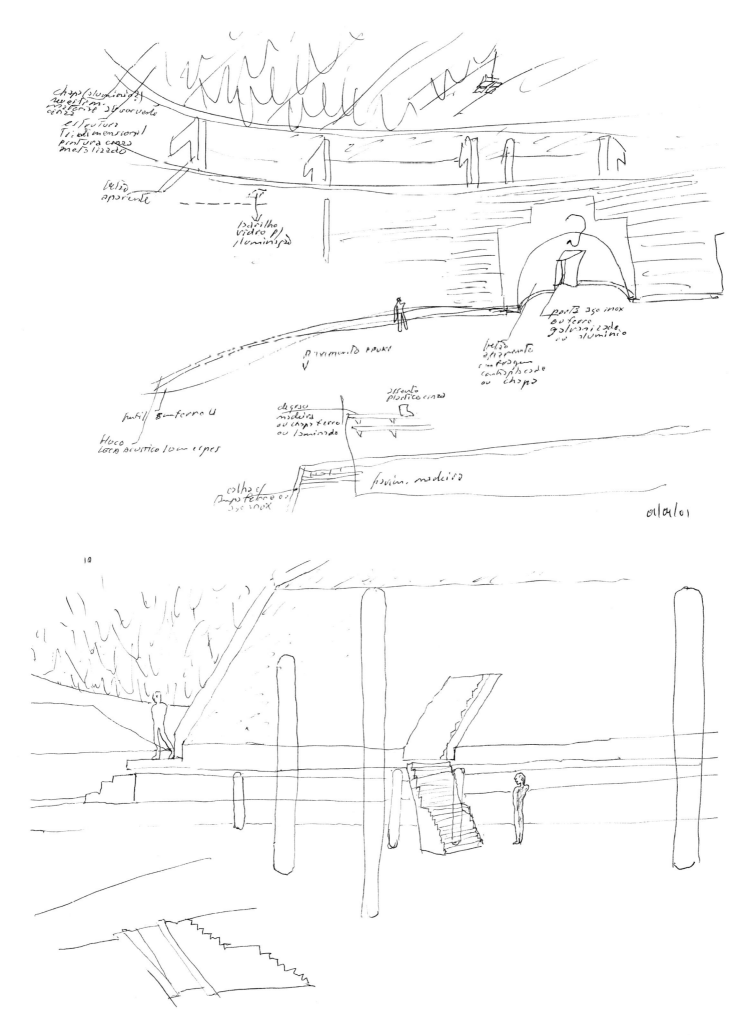

Above: Aerial view of the
pavilion from the southwest.

Opposite: Views of the pavilion
entrance canopy.

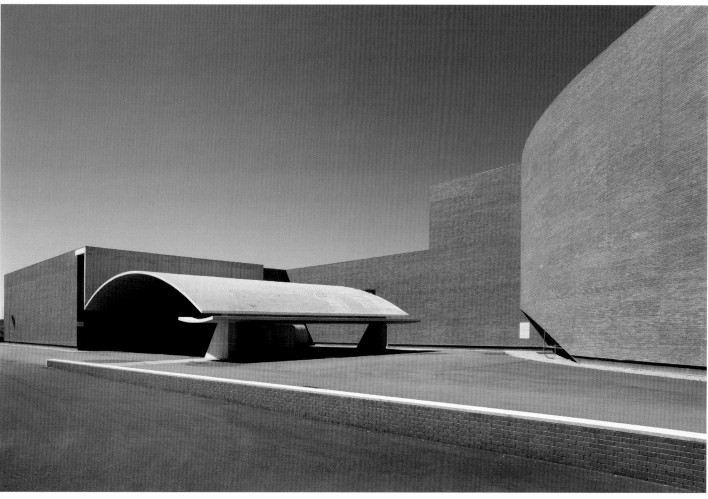

Multipurpose Pavilion

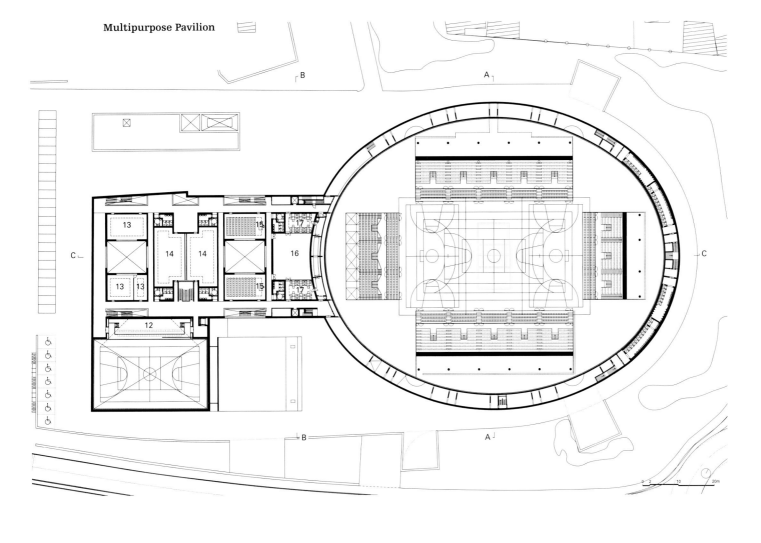

First-floor plan

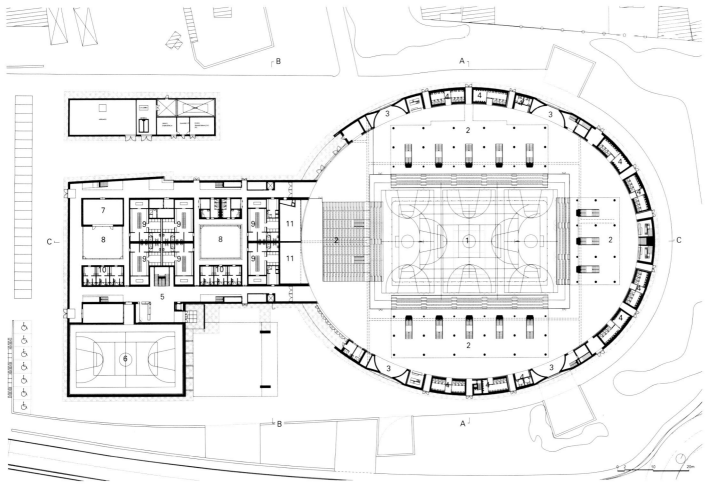

Ground-floor plan

1   Main field
2   Spectator stand
3   Emergency exit
4   Lavatory
5   Reception
6   Warm-up field
7   Weight room
8   Yard
9   Athlete's dressing room
10 Referee's dressing room
11 Storage
12 Bench
13 Administration area
14 VIP/Press room
15 Auditorium
16 Esplanade
17 Café

Section A

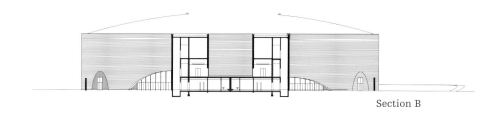

Section B

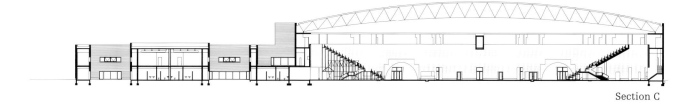

Section C

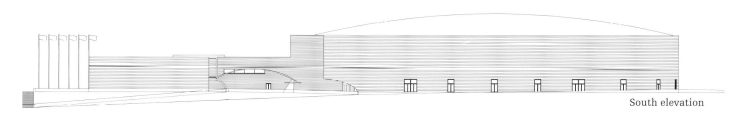

South elevation

0 2   10   20m

Opposite: Entrance to the sporting hall.

Below: Interior of sporting hall, with seating rows to the left and concave exit doors to the right.

115

Opposite above: Seating and
perimeter wall.
Opposite below: Entrance to
the spectator stands.

Below: Playing field area.

117

A mark on the land

'Take a right at the first roundabout, a left at the second, then cross the motorway and it's just there ahead of you: the bullfighting arena. You can't miss it', said the taxi driver as I was looking for the new multipurpose pavilion in Gondomar, which was then in its final stages of construction.

There are certain types of service buildings for which we don't seem to expect any architectural quality. Among them are sports facilities and in particular those called 'sports pavilions'. A hangar that looks like a codfish warehouse, shoved in the middle of a school, a town, or an urban or suburban neighbourhood seems to be enough to keep the local authority, the sporting and recreational club, or the school happy. As well as the general population, it seems. Perhaps if that were the case with the new pavilion in Gondomar, or maybe if it had a cool modern look, the taxi driver would have infused his information with pride.

What I've said here about sports pavilions might also be said of other facilities of a public nature, such as schools, hospitals, health centres and markets. This is almost to say that, to the state – which is responsible in the majority of instances for the construction of such buildings – the only thing that matters is functionality. In most cases this is generally poor, precisely because of the lack of other elements. Due to the sheer rarity of the occasion, when an architect designs a sports pavilion, a school, a hospital or a market, that in itself is something special.

Lately, a few cultural facilities have been built (houses of culture, theatres, museums, foundations, libraries) with a concern for quality (certainly to be praised) that is not seen in hospitals, sports pavilions or markets. That demonstrates a certain definition of culture, which in my view is short-sighted, because it distorts and subdivides culture. As if there could possibly be a true cultural policy without quality spaces and good hospital care, without good facilities and a balanced leisure and sports component to life, without proper school buildings and sound pedagogical practice.

Siza has designed for Gondomar a multipurpose pavilion that is an exception to this rule. Albeit a mere recreational-sporting facility, it has the dignity of a cultural centre or of a library. It sits at the exit of the A29 motorway and is immediately recognizable because of its dimension and its brick colour. Sitting in between a discontinuous rural landscape and that of an overbuilt town, the new building stakes out its own responsibilities: it puts its paws down, one elliptical, another rectangular, and marks its territory.

To mark, in this context, means to profess an affirmation, a 'yes!' with conviction, in the midst of a Babel of confused and hesitant languages. It signifies a choice, the placement of a grid which can filter, cut and interpret. That is, it opens a space for serious dialogue, which will generate the transformation of the land and of those who inhabit the area.

– Nuno Higino

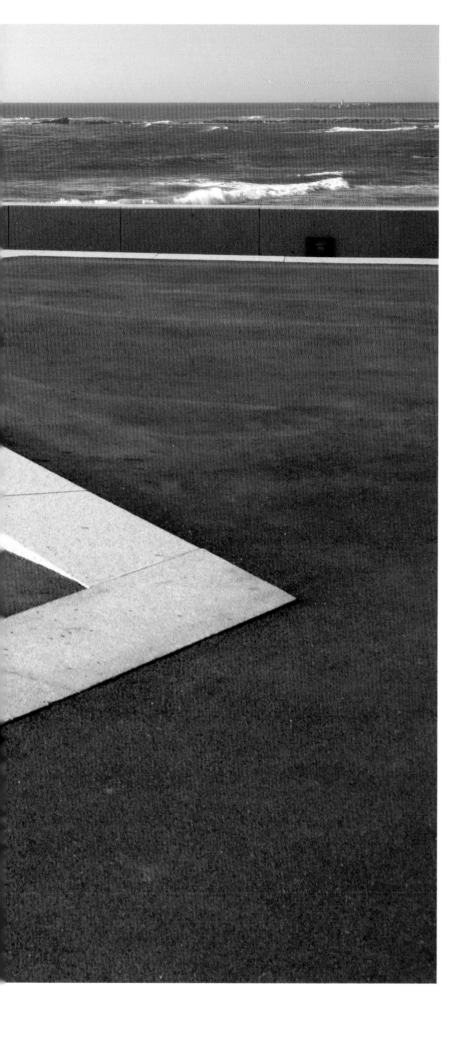

Masterplan for
Vila do Conde's coastal road
Vila do Conde, Portugal
2001–2007

Masterplan for Vila do Conde's coastal road

The plan for the work to this area of the coastal road was drawn up in coordination with the study for the area immediately north of it, which was prepared by the architect Alcino Soutinho. It is expected that our plan will in time be extended to the south. It consists of the following works:

– Repairing and cladding the supporting wall that limits the beach. This is constructed of 20 centimetres of Caverneira granite, capped by a low, 40-centimetre wall.
– Building a footpath and bicycle path along the low wall, in grey bituminous concrete with a granite curb.
– Creating planting on the existing dunes in-between the coastal promenade and Avenida do Brasil.
– Providing for pedestrian routes across the dunes. These are paved in grey bituminous concrete, which is cast in place between two low walls of exposed white concrete.
– Building car-parking bays at the eastern and western ends of the avenue, to accommodate 440 and 410 cars respectively, also paved in grey bituminous concrete with granite curbs.
– Repaving Avenida do Brasil in grey concrete.
– Replanting the flowerbeds, including new trees, at the eastern end of the avenue.
– Rebuilding all necessary infrastructural networks.
– Constructing new buildings to serve the area of the dunes in a location adjoining the pedestrian paths:
– A restaurant, 500 square metres.
– A coffee shop, also 500 square metres.
– A nightclub, 1,500 square metres.
– A 45 by 25 metre beach football pitch.
– A saltwater swimming pool and changing areas.
– A café and esplanade.

– Álvaro Siza

Sketches of seating and other interventions along the road.

Opposite: Views of the
path around the São João
Baptista fort.

Below: Walking path and paved
path beyond.

125

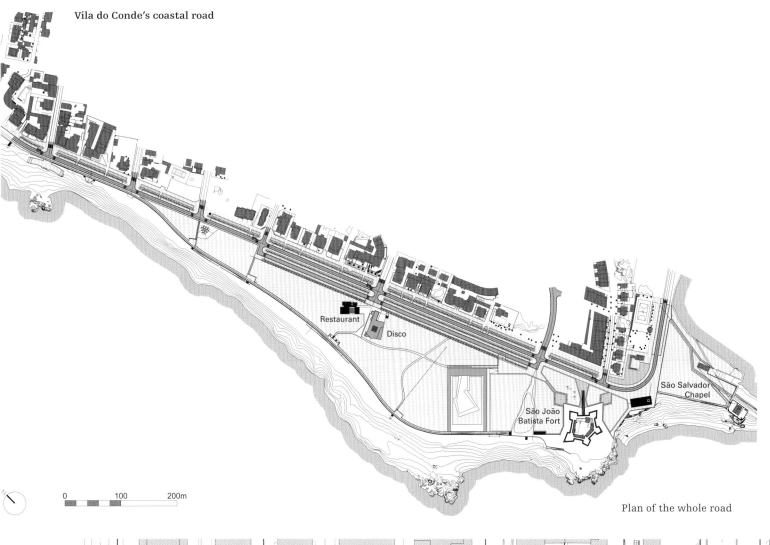

Vila do Conde's coastal road

Restaurant

Disco

São João
Batista Fort

São Salvador
Chapel

0   100   200m

Plan of the whole road

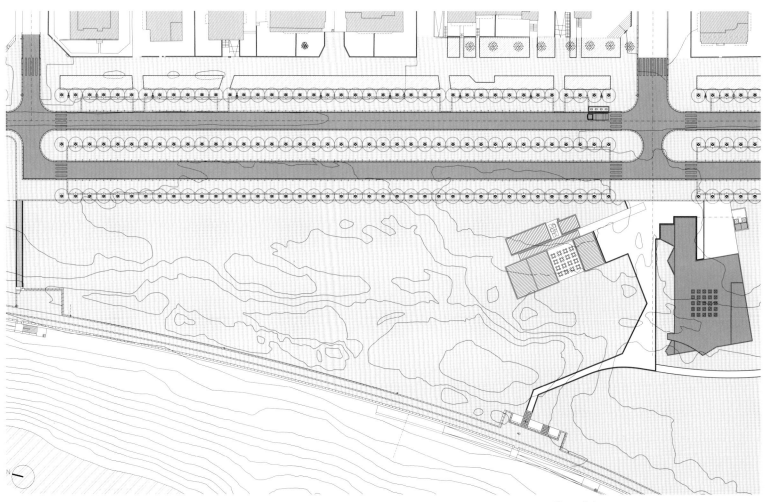

Plan of the restaurant

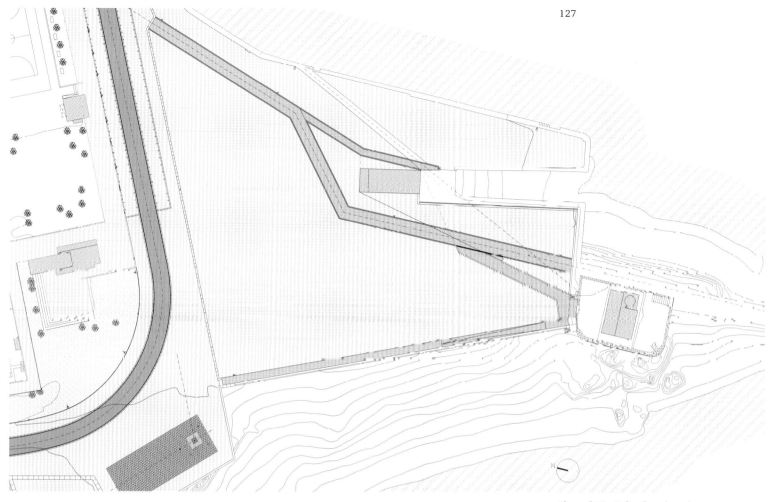

Plan of São Salvador chapel

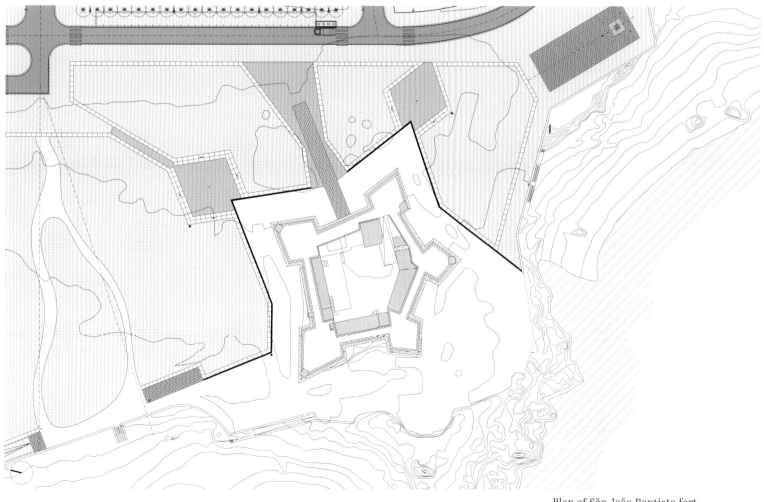

Plan of São João Baptista fort

Give history its dues

I park the car in Caxinas and walk along the new coastal road in the direction of Vila do Conde. The morning is a pleasant one, and there is an intermittent but continuous flow of pedestrians and cyclists. Here and there are the first swimmers: some lying on the sand, others crouching on the rocks like molluscs. Various ice-cream sellers are starting to set up their stalls. After walking for 15 minutes, I come to a split on the road: I choose the path closer to the sea, which ends by wrapping itself around the fort of São João Baptista, where it meets up with the route for vehicular traffic. Separating one path from the other, the dunes are still here. Every so often, a line connects the two. It appears that the plants on the dunes have been lifted and relocated; between grasses and shrubs, little blue, red and yellow flowers mark out landing strips for pigeons and other birds. What a pity that a fence is necessary to protect this colourful and wild carpet. I make my way around the fort, which has been cleaned and restored, and through the bustling surrounding area. At the bend on the road around the fort, where at other times you could hear the screeching of cars and smell the warm odour of burnt tyre, traffic now flows calmly.

It is about an hour now since I started out so I need an esplanade, a place for a coffee and a cigarette. As I sit down, I wonder, could we make an overall plan to preserve and order the Portuguese coastline? The area around this plan includes almost 5 kilometres of coastal road, from the boundary with Póvoa to as far as where the cod is dried, and includes a stretch where the way splits to produce two separate routes. What if they were connected to the other works already completed along the coast, to become a dignified boundary for this place where, in the words of poet Luís de Camões, 'land ends and the sea begins'?

As Portuguese, at the edge of the European continent, we have a responsibility to witness and honour this meeting (almost never a peaceful one) between the land and the sea. We are responsible for this meeting between the two, for the end and the beginning of each. I thought of a lecture titled 'The Other Cape', which Jacques Derrida gave in Turin in 1980 about Europe and its future. Europe is a cape, a protrusion of that immense continent which was Eurasia. We, the inhabitants of the extreme land of the edge of the cape, are about to fall into the sea. It is with something more than anticipation that we fall in, like the blind man stretching his hand ahead to meet hidden dangers first and protect his body. We go forth head first with all that pose entails: courage, on the one hand, and

irresponsibility (or even suicide), on the other.

Europe is like the western appendix of a great Asia. A small geographical cape, an advance post for a gigantic continent, but also the starting point for discovery, invention and colonization. A cape that has become a head, the centre for decision-making and cultural tutelage.

The Portuguese coastline is the limit, the extreme edge of that cape. In some ways, the edge remains out of mind. Not only is it the territorial edge, where land and sea come together and fight, but it is also the political, economic and strategic edge. Old Europe, burnt out to its extremity, is finding it hard to respond to its own memory. It is finding it hard to take on its responsibility, to bear witness to the universality that it has always fostered. Having given 'new worlds to the world', as Camões put it, Portugal must now risk looking to other capes, other capitals, other models of democracy, towards the opening of other frontiers that will necessarily establish other priorities, other paths, other edges.

We don't know what awaits us. Nobody knows. None the less, we have to protect that wait. That which we anticipate is by definition neither programmable nor predictable. We have to learn how to wait with vigilance and responsibility. Those whom we have kept under our dominance through the centuries that have gone by, those whom we subjugated, exploited or even destroyed in their own homes, are now knocking at our door: they arrive at the edge, they arrive outside of legality, language, culture and seem destined to be marginalized. But to look after the edge is not a marginal thing to do. It is an imperative, a responsibility. We know from history that the pressure that shakes the interior (of territories or of political, economic or ideological systems) is often applied from the edges.

All these things I thought about, sitting at the esplanade inside the bend at the fort. I had just walked the coastal road, reconfigured by Siza, and with a coffee and a cigarette, among half a dozen tourists from inland Europe who shared that sunny morning with me, I thought of the importance of edges and of marginal people, in the hope that there may be continuity to this work on the recovery of our coastline. It will be a way of giving history its dues.

– Nuno Higino

Views of the road and esplanade
near the São João Baptista fort.

Viana do Castelo Municipal Library
Viana do Castelo, Portugal
2001–2007

Viana do Castelo Municipal Library

The Viana do Castelo Municipal Library is built on a strip of land between the river Lima and Avenida Marginal. It forms part of the waterfront development plan produced by Fernando Távora. In addition to the library, the plan includes external landscaping, a multipurpose room, and two office buildings that frame the Praça da Liberdade and a monument to 25 April 1974, the day of the Revolution. The site for the library was agreed on with Távora and the other architects involved in the project (Eduardo Souto de Moura, José Bernardo Távora and Adalberto Dias).

Located at the eastern end of the planned row of buildings, the library consists of an elevated volume of 45 square metres, including a central void of 20 square metres. Only the east side of this volume extends fully to the ground, where it forms one leg of an L-shaped plan pointing eastwards. Low retaining walls, forming the waterfront landscaping, also extend to the east. Public access to the library atrium is through the space defined by the elevated volume and its central void. The ground floor is raised 0.65 metres above the ground, and can be reached by either a ramp or four steps. The staff can also access the library through this public courtyard, or via a covered area at the eastern end of the building, which has dimensions designed to accommodate the library's service truck. Adjacent to this area are the electricity substation and the boiler room.

The architectural expression is essentially the result of the following concerns:
- Views of the river Lima through a substantial area of the building. This is achieved by elevating most of the floor area, supporting it at the western end with two L-shaped piers, and at the eastern end by the construction of the ground-floor volume.
- Orthogonality in plan and elevation.
- The predominance of horizontal openings, complemented by skylights.
- Protection from the sun, and the appropriate orientation of the openings to achieve this.
- An exposed white concrete external surface, to be partially clad in faceted stone, which forms a base to the building.
- Volumetric definition deliberately conditioned by the dialogue between the garden and the building.

– Álvaro Siza

Sketch studying building form and centre void.

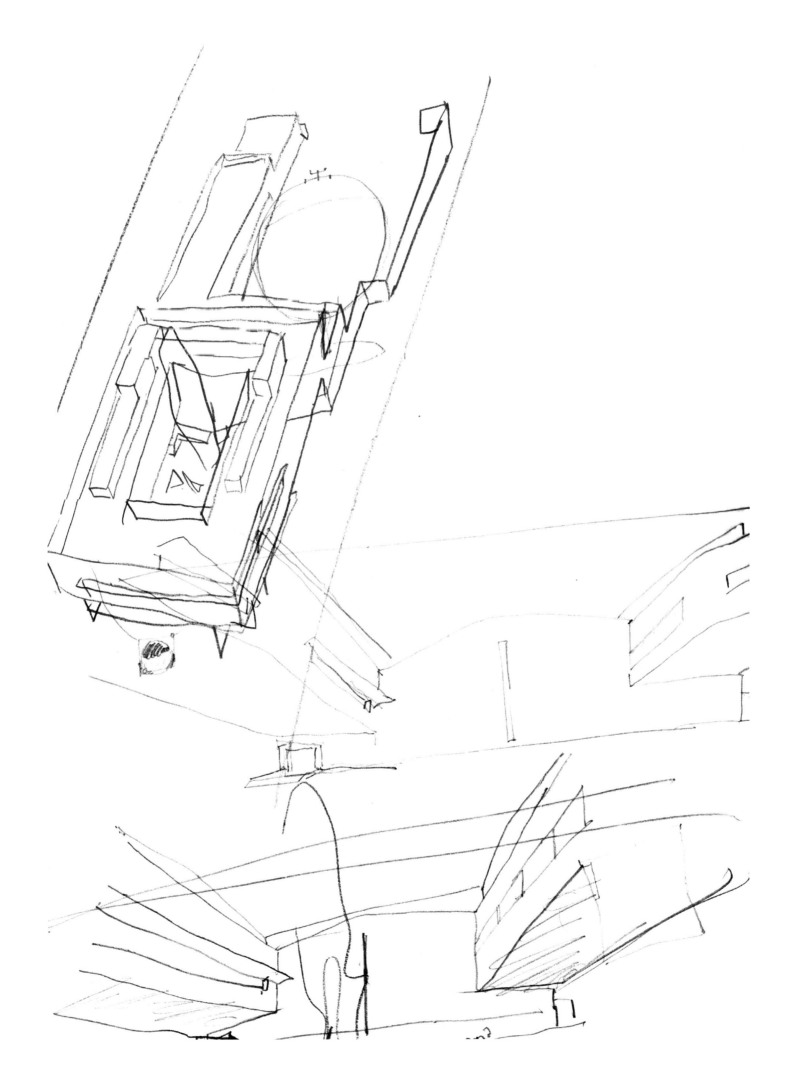

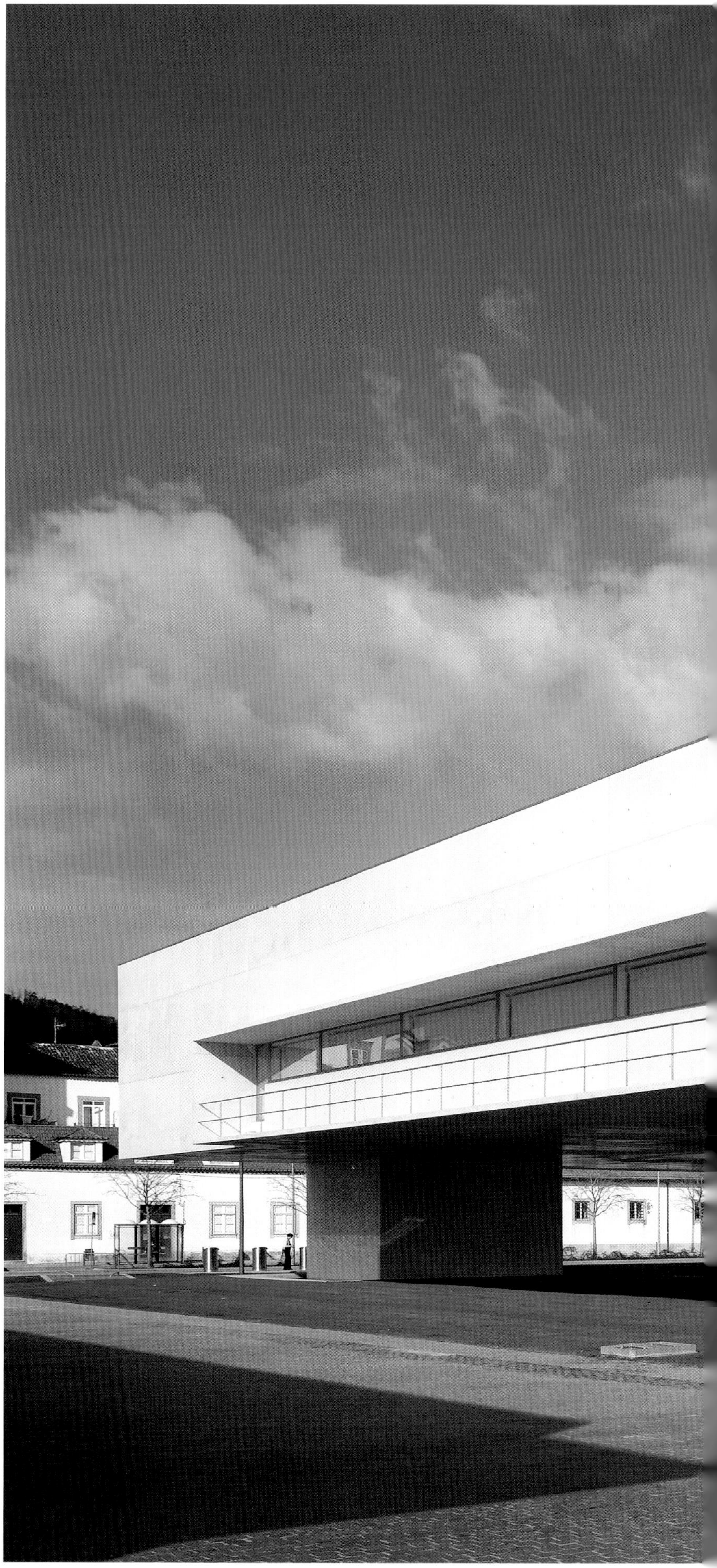

View of the library from
the south.

Section A

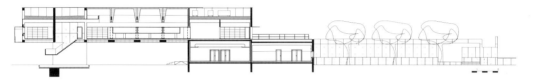

Section B

1 Foyer
2 Reception
3 Café
4 Storage
5 Multipurpose room
6 Technical services
7 Office
8 Meeting room
9 Computer search
10 Staff room
11 Reserve room
12 Book and media storage
13 Conservation room
14 Adult zone
15 Work room
16 Multimedia section
17 Audio/video section
18 Periodicals
19 Reading area
20 Room for European study
21 Self-education room
22 Children's zone
23 Story room
24 Expression workshop room
25 Toddler reading area
26 Juvenile reading area
27 Baby space
28 Balcony

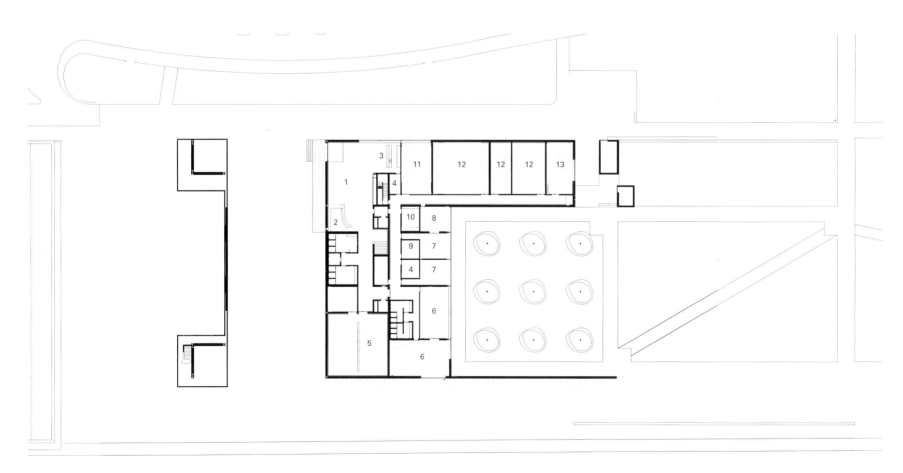

Ground-floor plan

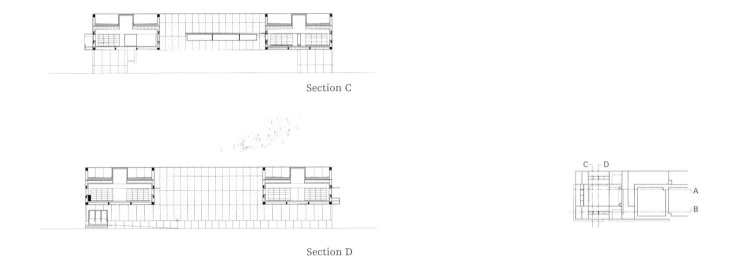

Section C

Section D

C D

A

B

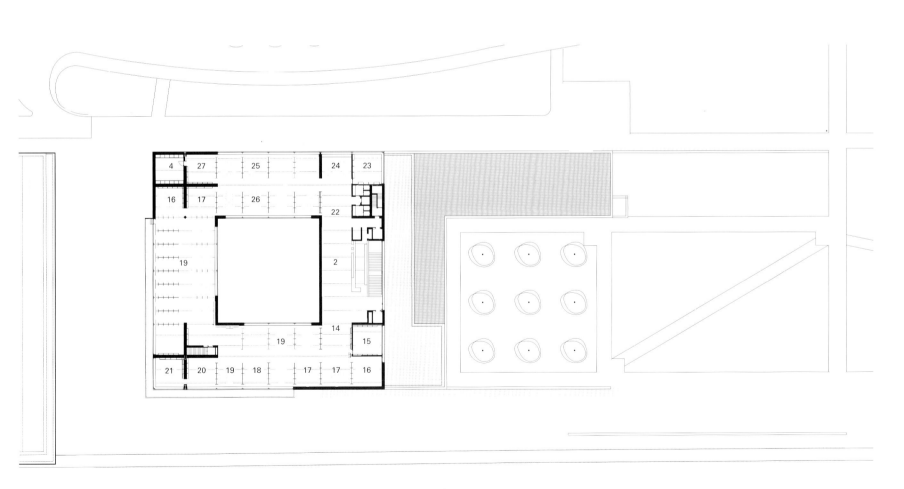

First-floor plan

Opposite: Deep sun shading over windows and structural pillars.

Below: Emergency stair, looking towards the river to the south.

141

View of the library from the river.

Between the river and the city

The construction of a network of national libraries, of which the library in Viana do Castelo is part, impacts on our reading habits but also the preservation and development of our historical and literary patrimony. A library is a place of memory. Not passive memory, but memory that is actively thrust forwards, in order to inform the future.

The building designed by Siza seems to understand this connection between that which is there already and that which is yet to come. Its volume is elevated above the ground, so as to get a better view of the river Lima, and also not to cut off the relationship between the building and the city. For a relationship to exist, a certain tension is necessary, and to create tension, supports are necessary. The lightness of the building fosters this relationship, between building and city. It provides support for looking, without either excessively determining one's gaze or obstructing it.

To build on a strip of land is to build between two frontiers, with all the limitations and dangers that such an endeavour implies. Any boundary generates tension, because its purpose is to protect heterogeneous and disparate interests. Inherent to any boundary are dangers, including contamination, threats to private property, abuse of power and the enforcement of the law of the strongest, as it is truly a 'no-man's land'. Frequently, when this boundary separates a city and a river, the city assaults the river, contaminates it, literally imposing its asymmetrical and tyrannical rules on the water. Sometimes the river reacts in an unruly fashion and causes disruption and damage to the city. The river and the city are territories of different natures.

In building between one and the other, Siza exposes himself to this tension. Pressured from both sides, he didn't avoid the conflict, but neither did he exacerbate it. Instead, Siza opened up a dialogue, without demagogy or false promises. Not overbearing, not exorbitant, not talking too loud, the building is indifferent to neither river nor city. It doesn't fall into submission. Although surrounded (perhaps even besieged), it resists and states its position. It conquers a place – its place – on the frontier. It arrives and says simply, here I am, this is the place that was destined for me, now we all have to live together.

Between the lines of this new library in Viana there is a subtext that can be read: it takes effort and the ability to interpret.

– Nuno Higino

Opposite: View under the
southwest side of the
elevated square.

Below: Sun-shade on the
southwest side of the building.

145

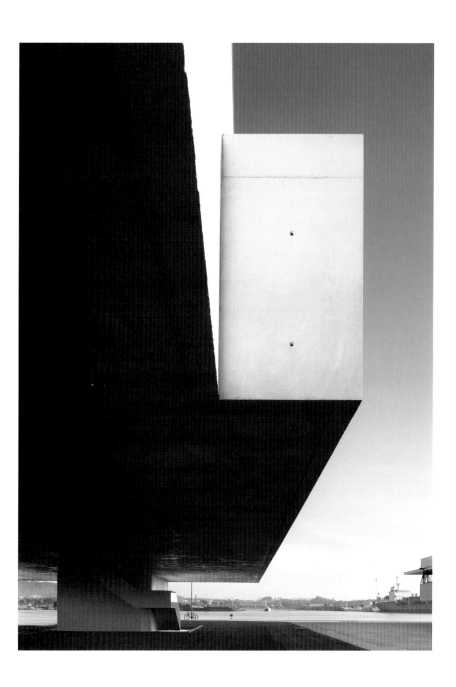

Above: Exterior void at night.

Opposite: Library interior with skylights and view to the river.

Masterplan for
Leça da Palmeira's coastal road
Matosinhos, Portugal
2002–2007

Masterplan for Leça da Palmeira's coastal road

Leça da Palmeira's coastal road, Avenida da Liberdade, is the location for two of our office's important early projects, the Marés ocean swimming pool (1961–66) and the Tea House and Chapel of the Boa Nova restaurant (1958–63). It consists of two 6-metre-wide thoroughfares, separated by a central band, interrupted by crossroads controlled by traffic lights. This design is intended to create a more disciplined traffic flow and a reduction in vehicular speed, in keeping with the change in character that was sought for the thoroughfare, from a road to a street.

To the west of the avenue, along the beach and over an existing oil pipeline, a pedestrian promenade has been built, paved with a surface conducive to jogging, skating, and cycling, and lined with *metrosideros* (a species of trees that will withstand the aggression of the maritime conditions). The pavement allows for the inclusion of access chambers to the underground oil pipeline, and can be easily opened in the case of an emergency need for direct access. Resting areas with stone benches are located along the promenade at the principal access points to the beach, at the pedestrian crossings, and at the location of other important services.

The existing vehicular access to the Chapel and Tea House of Boa Nova was discontinued and substituted with access along the north side of the lighthouse. Existing pedestrian paths around the monument to António Nobre were also rearranged. We proposed a redesign of the junction between Rua Belchior Robles and the north end of the avenue, as far as the crossroads known as *o Rochedo* (the Rocky), which will now have two-way traffic and a separating band, as envisaged for the southern end of the avenue. At this end of the avenue, the Statutory Guidelines for Coastal Planning have been adopted in order to site the car-parking areas, which will be restricted to pockets located to the west of the avenue. At the southern end of the avenue, parking is organized in bays and limited to specific areas along both thoroughfares. These include two vacant sites facing the beach in Leça, which were previously occupied by the army, and the strip that will be freed up when the current oil pipelines are disconnected.

The choice of finishes and cladding materials was based on parameters of economy and durability. We looked for materials that would not require substantial upkeep and which will retain a good appearance as they age. So the roadway is coated in tarmac, the curbs are granite, the parking bays are paved in granite cubes, the promenade and footpaths in bituminous material and the resting points in granite slabs. Public lighting is achieved predominantly by 15-metre-tall projectors placed in the traffic separation band. These shed light uniformly along the avenue and supplementary lighting is added at the stopping points.

– Álvaro Siza

Aerial view of the road.

Leça da Palmeira's coastal road

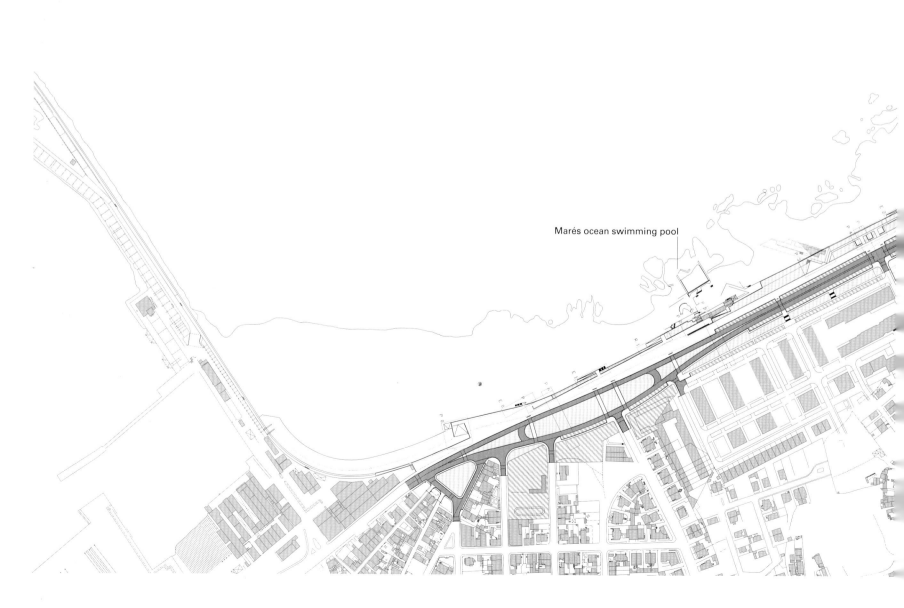

Marés ocean swimming pool

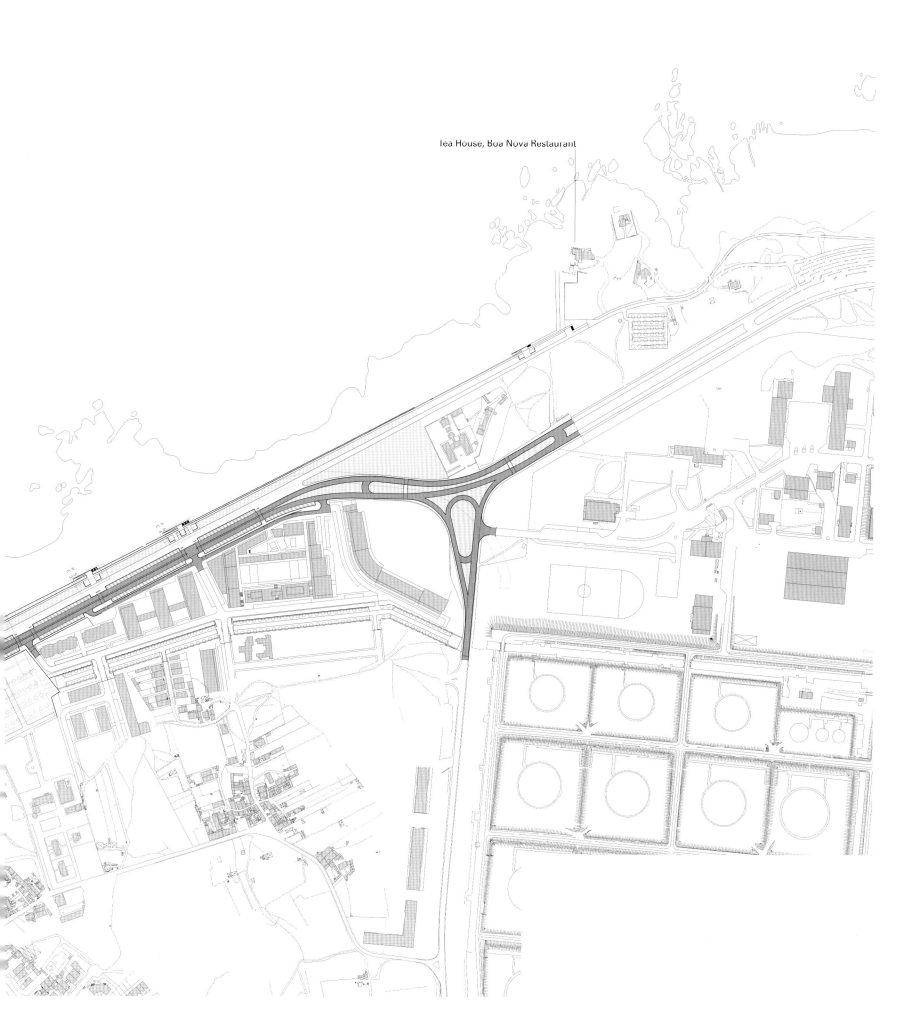

Tea House, Boa Nova Restaurant

Because the sea is what matters

A coastal road is not a picnic area. It is a place of movement: walking, running, skating, riding on a tricycle or a bicycle. A place that is continually being made. To get to know the coastal road in Leça da Palmeira it is necessary to enter that movement, to be there at the weekend and witness the circulation of the crowd. A coastal road is not made from elaborate conceptual speculations, nor from enigmatic opinions, nor is it a product of local issues (which are currently so prevalent). It is made of stone, asphalt, grass, traffic lights, cars both stationary and moving, the sound of horns, animals leashed and unleashed, carts selling ice-cream and sweets, esplanades, chit-chat, confiding, flirting. It is also made of opinion, critique, and civic intervention. For that very reason, it would be legitimate to expect that those who put up protest banners against the asphalt, or who demanded palm trees and garden benches, should protest with the same vehemence against the construction of yet another café-bar on the sand.

A coastal road is also made of that which is to come, of the inventive thinking of those who can transform it into an even livelier place. The coastal road has always been a road on the coast. What truly transformed it was an apparently simple ordering of the elements, the materials, the functions and the routes. Although this transformation is not irrevocable, for any intervention in this territory – whatever it may be – is only yet another layer over an impossible-to-saturate palimpsest. But now the sea, the rocks, the sand, the sea air, the great ships in the distance and the fishing boats nearer to the coast, even the winds, all appear more clearly in their relationship with the lines of the horizon and that of the coast.

With the planet's global warming and the consequent rise in sea level, we don't know what this (and other) coastal roads may become in a few years' time. In a way, it doesn't matter. Both time and man will take it upon themselves to strike new boundaries from those determined by nature. At the moment, the coastal road in Leça is a place full of life and potential. The 'true' coastline (if any such thing ever exists) is still to be invented, or reinvented. Even generations and generations of architects, yet to be born, will not find it.

– Nuno Higino

Opposite above: Paved path and grass provide for recreation.
Opposite below: Frequent crosspaths help control traffic.

House in Pego
Sintra, Portugal
2002–2007

House in Pego

The site for this house is large – over 20 square metres – and it lies on a sea-facing slope with a north–northwest orientation and a substantial fall in level from approximately 105 metres to 70 metres. The building sits on a relatively level platform on the higher part of the site, and enjoys magnificent views over Praia das Maçãs and Praia Grande.

The building contains five bedrooms, a small study, a large living room and a kitchen. Each part is arranged as a semi-independent element along an internal route that connects the whole house, from the external reception space at one end to the most private accommodation at the other. The intersections of these semi-autonomous elements with the interior gallery define several irregular external spaces, creating semi-private patios that are open to the landscape.

The internal gallery, which is also irregular in shape, is illuminated by openings directly to the outside, creating special stopping points along the route. Although organized as a single storey, the building actually has four different levels, each corresponding approximately to the external level at that point in its sequence.

The building is constructed of load-bearing masonry, clad in treated timber, with timber windows and a concrete slab roof covered with metal sheeting. As this is the client's second home, the finishes are as simple as possible, giving special emphasis to the quality of the spatial organization. Outside the house itself, a covered area for car-parking and an open-air swimming pool complete the brief.

– Álvaro Siza

Opposite: Sketches of the building's form and relation to the landscape.

Above: Facade, showing the
privacy of each block.

Opposite: View to the sea
from the roof (top) and the
house (below).

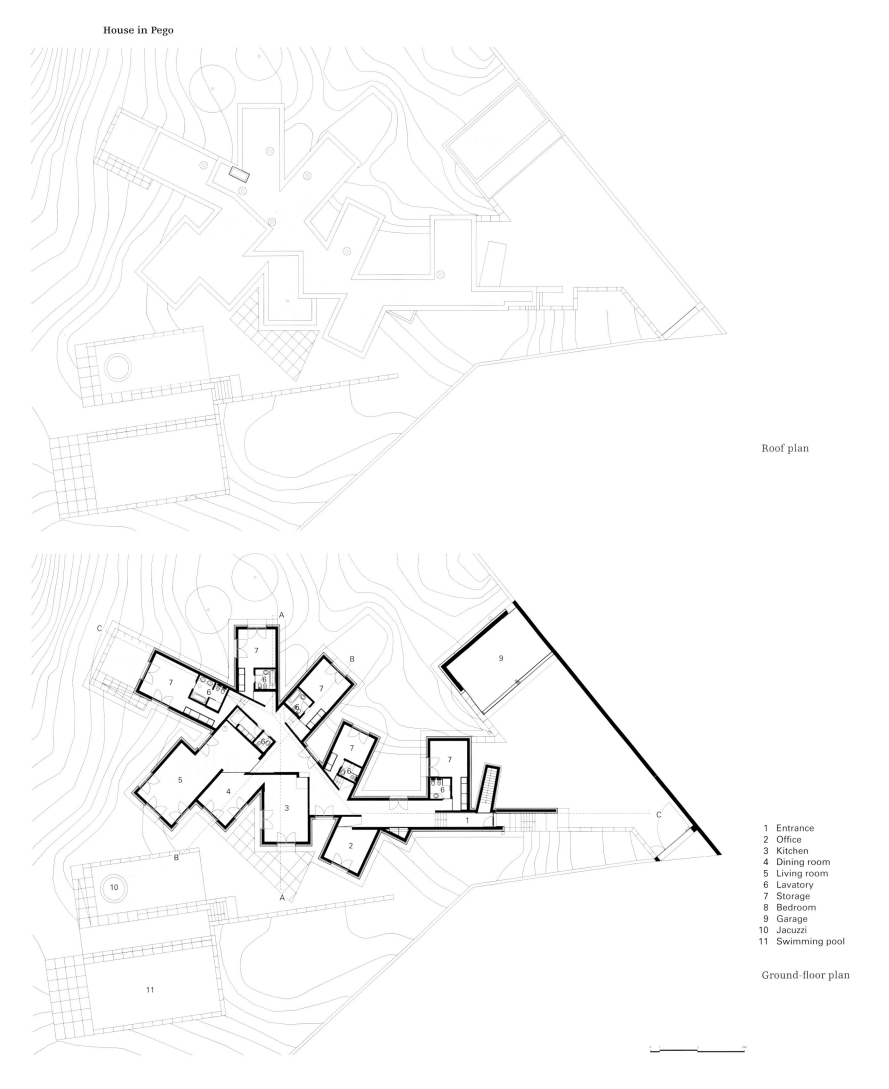

Roof plan

Ground-floor plan

1 Entrance
2 Office
3 Kitchen
4 Dining room
5 Living room
6 Lavatory
7 Storage
8 Bedroom
9 Garage
10 Jacuzzi
11 Swimming pool

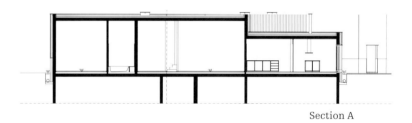

Section A

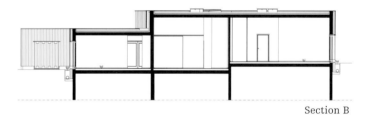

Section B

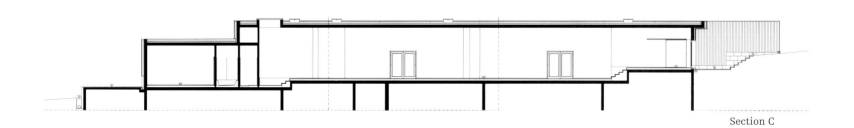

Section C

Opposite above: House seen from the swimming pool. Opposite below: Main entrance to the house.

Below: Living room and dining room.

165

A good plan always produces a good elevation

My first contact with the House in Pego was a casual one. On the wall of the meeting room of Siza's office was, and maybe still is, a drawing that reminded me of a flower. A stem, leaves on the stem, and petals. A freehand drawing in heavy lines, or maybe a photocopy of a drawing that was enlarged, as Siza does when he wants to – needs to – flirt with something, some indecision. And there it is, he goes on looking, seeing, looking again, then ignoring it, then giving it the attention that it requires and that is possible.

The drawing intrigued me but at the time I wasn't able to establish what it depicted. It could have been a theme for a rug, because it shared wall space with drawings for rug designs, not to mention site photographs, working drawings, enlarged sketches, Saint Paul falling off his horse, a sketch for the tiled wall panel at the new basilica in Fatima. A miscellany of things in an organized mess, some of which gets periodically cleared away, allowing others, by virtue of necessity or delay, to come to the fore as an overlay on top of the permanent ones.

The flower was the plan for a house in Sintra, which was already being constructed under the supervision of Siza's collaborator for this project, architect António Madureira. The drawing surprised and intrigued me, but I wasn't able to investigate it further at that moment. The organization of that plan was, and is, just like that of a plant. Circulation is through the stem, as far out as the petals and back from the petals to the stem. I didn't recall having seen anything in Siza's work similar to this arrangement. It intrigued me.

Organizing exhibitions of Siza's work, as well as publishing or collaborating on publications, forces and enables me to keep up to date with what Siza is building, designing and sketching. This is not easy because, apart from his own office, Siza has other centres of production, such as the offices of António Madureira, Rogério Cavaca, Eduardo Souto de Moura, my own and others. Both necessity and opportunity obliges me to know what Siza is doing.

When I went to Sintra, the flower – that is, the house – was ready. It was still missing a garden, just as important for a house as it is for a flower. Seeing the completed project, my surprise was even greater than when I had seen the flower plan on the wall. This is Siza: the surprise of Siza, the irony of Siza, who is always present and cutting-edge, making it impossible to categorize his work.

Often – almost always – we need to categorize, to reference a building by means of its use of materials, form, organization, type and morphology. When we think that we have a catalogue of Siza's works or his method, he disappoints us by breaking with the stereotypes and formulae, which are necessary for our categorization. But this disappointment is inspirational. These changes are not done for the sake of rupture or gratuitous irreverence, but for the pleasure of creation, and the new work is always calm and cohesive even when it is dazzling.

This house is very simple. It has one access point and a number of volumes along a connecting route. To put it another way, a bunch of volumes or spaces are overlaid, distributed about a dynamic centre as they try to determine their own function, their turn in the sun. There is a hierarchy of spaces, of functions, of volumes, which conforms to a natural logic. Then we have the materials, in particular the external timber cladding, which almost seems fashionable as it is so often used these days. Except that here there is something different, not so common, but actually common in a work by Siza, which is the masterly use of this one material along with others. Everything is in its given place, in accordance with the rules, but then there are exceptions, playful gestures, which when controlled enrich the simple forms.

The House in Pego is a baffling piece of work, in which the humour of its creator is evident. It is joyful. It is a pity that it is a private building and therefore not accessible to the public, for everyone deserves to see it.

– Carlos Castanheira

House in Mallorca
Palma de Mallorca, Spain
2002–2007

House in Mallorca

This project is a summer home located in Mallorca, an island in the Mediterranean Sea. The site's main feature is its steep slope towards the sea. Access is from the northwest at the site's highest point, some 26 metres above sea level. Inspired by the surrounding rocky landscape, the project takes on a fragmented volumetric composition, spreading over the slope towards the sea. The overall volume is divided into three great blocks, which are then subdivided into smaller components. Composed of two levels above ground and one underground, each block is integrated into the existing topography by means of a platform built at 22 metres above sea level. Connections between separate volumes are achieved via passageways at different heights.

The main entrance to the house is located at the crossing of the platform with the central point of the east block, at the 22-metre level. The east block contains, in addition to this entrance, the master bedroom, a guest bedroom and a staircase. The west block is located between the east and north blocks, and acts as a central volume, spreading horizontally in order to connect the other two blocks at ground-floor level (18.6 metres).

The west block has three bedrooms in its upper floor (at 22.10 metres). These bedrooms close upon themselves, creating a light well, in an upwards vertical movement, connecting with a patio on the lower level. Adjacent to this patio is a living room, in which all the openings are oriented to the patio, negating any visual contact with the sea. This tension between the proximity of the sea and the impossibility of seeing it generates an introspective feeling in this room. This emphasizes the views over sea and land from other rooms of the house. The north block is a housekeeper's house, composed of a living room and two other rooms. Despite its functional simplicity, this volume takes on an important role as a fundamental element within the overall configuration.

– Álvaro Siza

Sketches showing the house's relationship to the landscape.

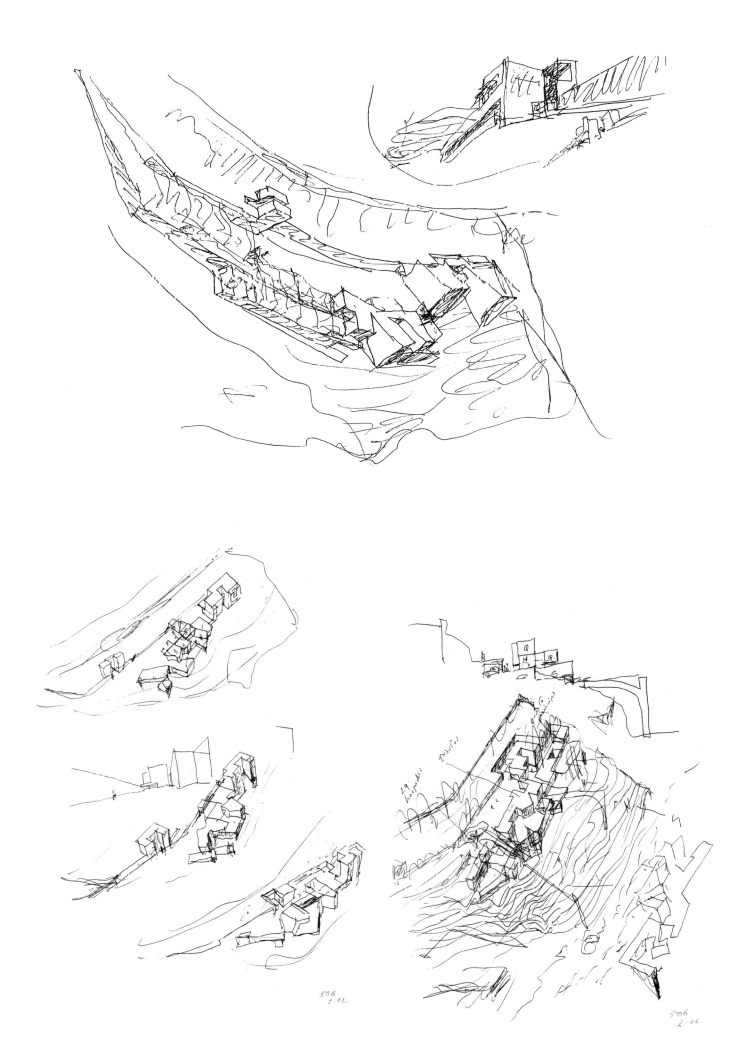

506
8.02

506
2.02

House in Mallorca

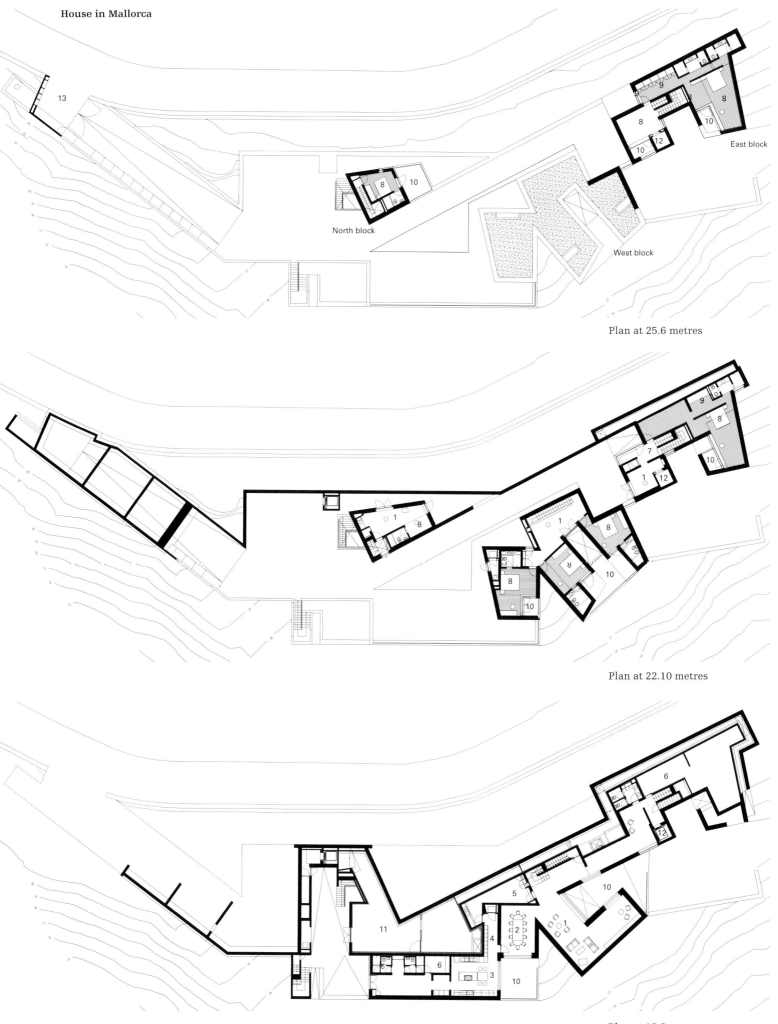

13

North block

West block

East block

8

9

8

10

8

12

10

Plan at 25.6 metres

9

8

7

1

12

10

1

8

1

8

8

8

10

10

Plan at 22.10 metres

6

7 2

5

10

11

4

1

2

6

3

10

Plan at 18.6 metres

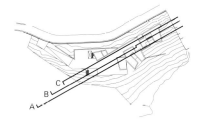

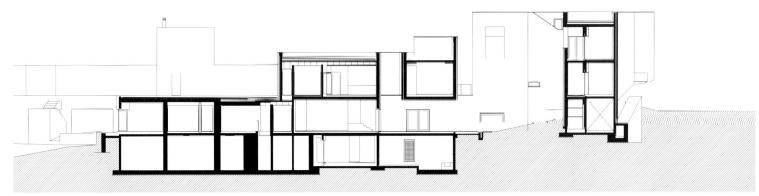

Section A

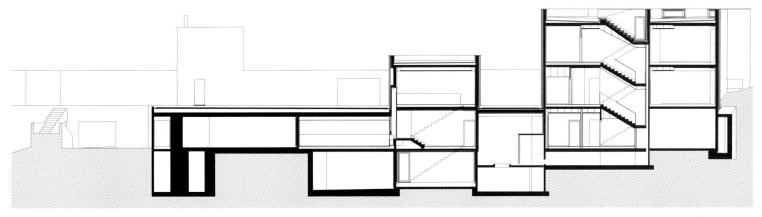

Section B

1 Living room
2 Dining room
3 Kitchen
4 Pantry
5 Storage
6 Vestibule
7 Hall
8 Bedroom
9 Closet
10 Terrace
11 Technical space
12 Lift
13 Driveway

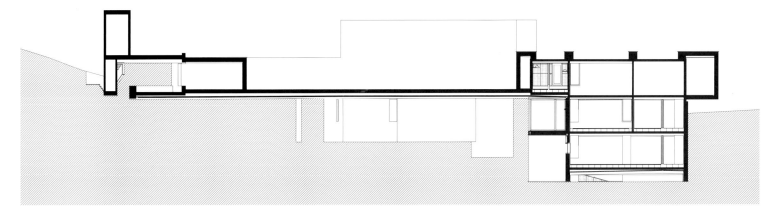

Section C

Above: East and west blocks
seen from the east.

Opposite: West block, seen from
the entrance to the house (top)
and roofs of all three blocks,
seen from the east block.

Opposite: Balcony outside
upper-level living room in the
west block.

Below: View from the terrace
outside the bedrooms on the
upper level of the west block.

181

Opposite: Entrance to the house (top) and view west, towards the north block on the patio level.

Below: View towards entry of east block.

183

What does a 'house' mean nowadays?

The idea of a 'house' contains many other ideas. Within tradition, there are two notions that seem essential to me: the idea of dwelling and the idea of property (which can be direct or indirect as well as temporary or permanent). A house is a place to dwell. Typically one person, or a community of people, make it their abode. Dwelling implies permanence, shelter, security and solicitude. One who dwells in a house takes care of it, is in charge of it and looks after its conservation and good order. We don't usually refer to people dwelling in an office block, or a school, a hospital or a factory. People are in these buildings for a given number of hours, which may even amount to more than the time they spend at home, but they do not dwell there. Even in cases where the distinction is less clear, it is difficult to associate the term 'house' with some places of long-term or even definitive permanence, such as retirement homes or prisons. As previously mentioned, the idea of a 'house' also entails the notions of property and ownership. Even people renting a house acquire rights over it and become 'owners' (even if only in limited ways), as certain rights and obligations are conferred on them by the actual owner.

Modern life has in many ways broken away from these concepts. The house is no longer a place of permanent life and activity, all day, all year, year after year, until inherited and preserved by a descendant who continues its lifeline. The contemporary house is locked up all day long, uninhabited. It is only at the end of the day that it is opened and acquires life: the house becomes sleeping quarters. Social mobility and volatility in the property market necessitates constant adaptation, adjustment and change. A 'house for life' nowadays is something of a rarity. The most common dwelling type, the flat or apartment, also contributes to the erosion of the notion of dwelling as it has been fostered by our social, cultural and architectural tradition.

This house in Mallorca is a holiday home, for sporadic and temporary occupation. It is a second home, a supplementary home, a place which, although it does not entirely shed the aura of dwelling, does distance itself from it. The three buildings that constitute this small complex find their space in-between the pine trees and discreetly open on to the sea. Each of the volumes folds in upon itself, screw-like, with an attitude of respect for the surrounding landscape, so that the magic is not broken, and the gaze may not tire of beauty. But beauty also tires: routine, a repeated view of the same, can draw down veils, cataracts over the eyes.

– Nuno Higino

View from the terrace of the west block.

House in Mallorca

Below: View of the west block from the pool terrace on the lower level.

Opposite: View of the east block.

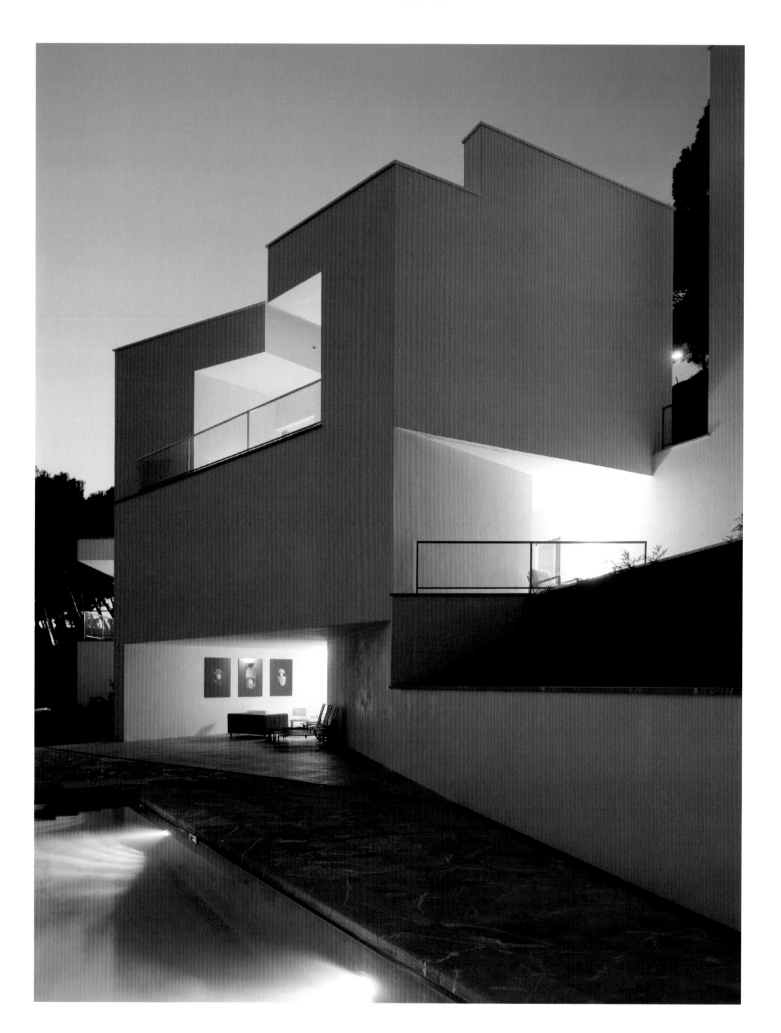

Living room in the lower level of
the west block. All openings are
oriented to an enclosed light shaft.

Institute of Educational Sciences
Cappont Campus,
University of Lleida,
Lleida, Spain
2002–2008

Institute of Educational Sciences

This project is located at the northeastern corner of Lleida University's Cappont Campus, which is in an extensive valley of old vegetable gardens on the river Segre.

The building is an L-shape that extends on the ground floor to form a U-shape. This extension creates the northern arm of the building, which serves to separate it from the large volume of the university library to the west while maintaining a coherent northern facade for the campus as a whole. This U-shape also surrounds a public square at its centre, which provides access to the other buildings on campus.

The ground floor of the west wing houses the administration and management services for the faculty. At the internal corner of the L-shape, the two main access routes to the building – one from the square and one from a pedestrian campus path – come together, and the main entry hall and principal vertical circulation node are located here. From this area, a ramping corridor leads to the north wing where the larger rooms are located, including music rooms, the examination hall and the gym.

The plans of the three upper floors are virtually the same, creating a strict repetition of functions and spaces. The east always contains offices for the various departments, and the west wing always houses classrooms. This consistency ensures a fluidity of circulation, which moves through linear galleries in the centre of each wing. Here, voids run vertically between all three floors, spreading natural light obtained from skylights and also providing a visual continuity that unifies the complex.

– Álvaro Siza

Sketch study of interior corner of L-shape.

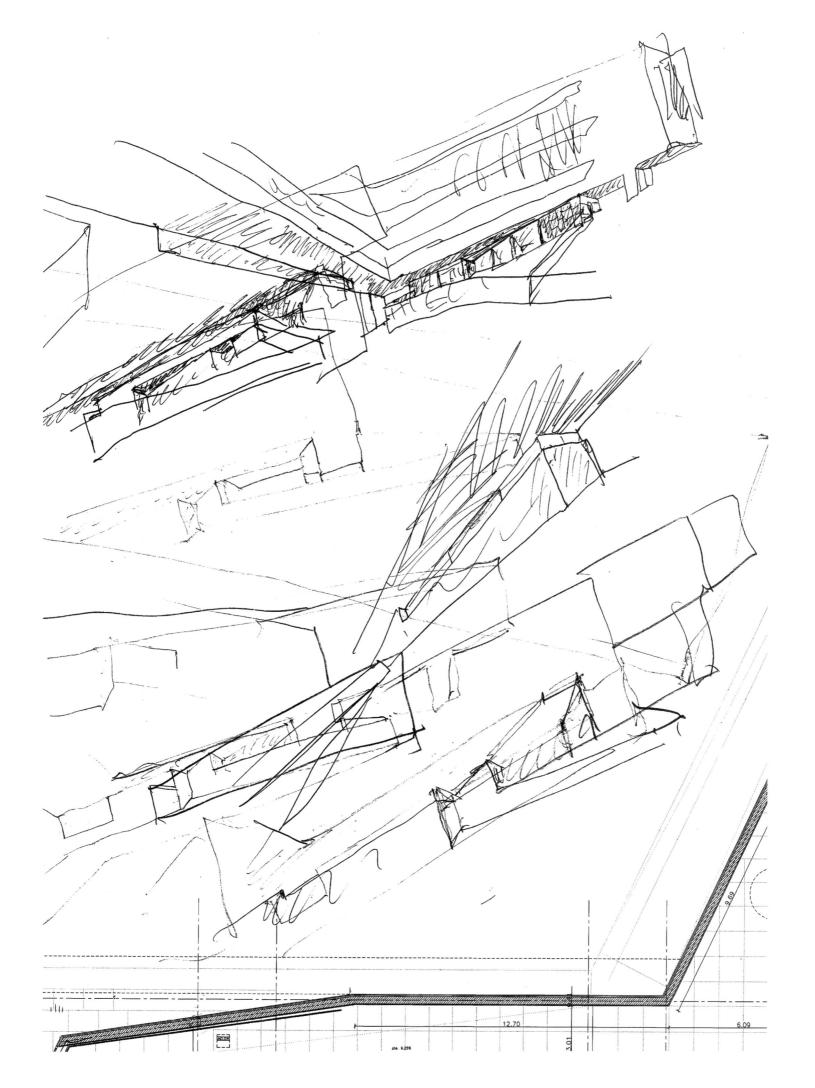

ple 9.25%   12.70   3.01   6.09

Institute of Educational Sciences

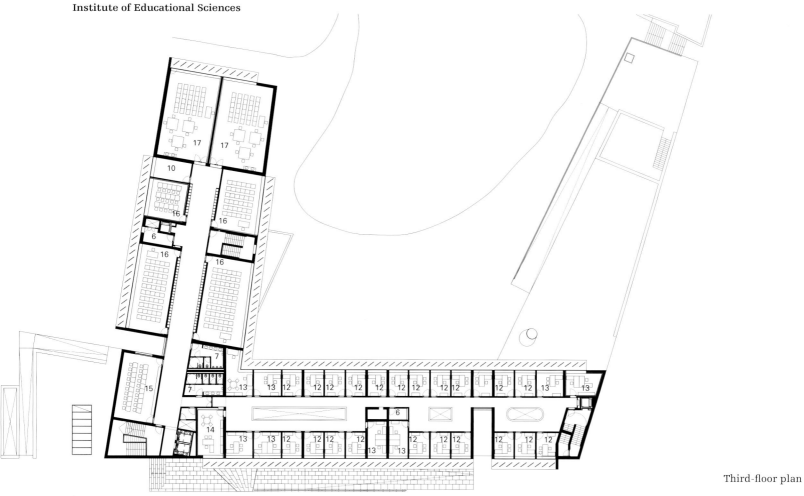

Third-floor plan

1 Lobby
2 Reception
3 Administrative office
4 Archive
5 Copy centre
6 Equipment room
7 Lavatories
8 Music classroom
9 Examination hall
10 Storage
11 Gymnasium
12 Individual office
13 Shared office
14 Communication area
15 Seminar room
16 Language lab
17 Classroom
18 Workshop classroom

Ground-floor plan

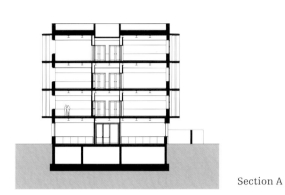

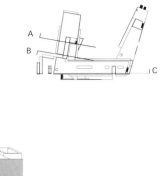

Section A

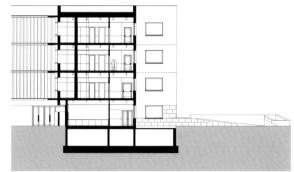

Section B

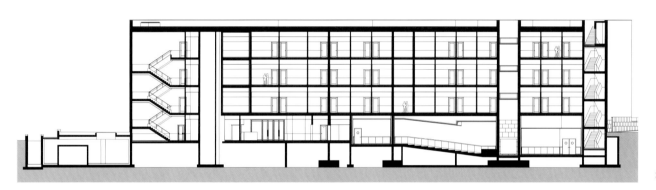

Section C

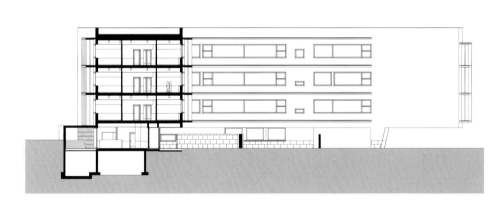

Section D

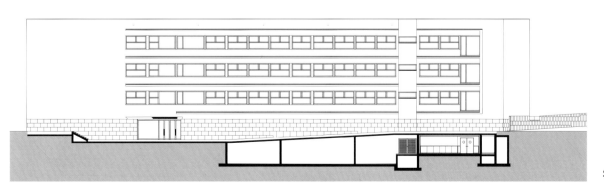

Section E

Below: Skylight above the main staircase, located at the internal corner of the L-shape.

Opposite: Skylight and light well on the third floor of the south wing.

Light well seen from the
second floor (above) and
ground floor (opposite).

All different, all the same

A school is a place for learning and for personal development. It is also a place for teaching and a place to live. Truly it is a house (or sometimes houses) of learning. Siza has built many schools, each a building in which to learn, to develop, to live and to be: the Teacher's Training College in Setúbal, the Faculty of Architecture at Porto University, the João de Deus Kindergarten in Peñafiel, the Library at the Aveiro University, the Faculty of Media Science at Santiago de Compostela University and the Institute of Educational Sciences at Lleida University. They are all different, and they are all the same.
They are different from so many others because it is politically unusual to invest in quality. This is because quality is not understood strategically, and it is also because those who are in charge of deciding whether to build schools did not, for the most part, go to school in buildings that had (or have) quality.
A school is made not only of teachers and pupils. The quality and commitment of both is essential, but if the space where they live, study and discuss is of no quality, or is in a state of disrepair, the experience is compromised. Something is missing and development remains incomplete.
A school designed and built by Siza is a house, albeit a large house, which takes as its basis the needs of a family, albeit a large family, suggesting potential organizations, generating life, comfort and confrontation. An interesting exercise is to visit, on the same day, Siza's Faculty of Architecture and his João de Deus Kindergarten, and then go to Santiago de Compostela for a walk through the Faculty of Media Science. Different times, different clients, but the same architect, and the same timeless quality of architecture. The spaces are timeless, as are the walls, whether in light or its shade.
As time moves on, changes and new technologies are required, but nothing should disturb the house, just as in our own homes. New appliances and new technologies arrive and we adapt. But the space and the quality remain the same, generous and magnificent. This space itself teaches, it demonstrates, and its lessons are passed on even to the most insensitive of students and teachers, because there is a difference between a disordered space in disrepair and an ordered space in good condition. Quality is the reason for quantity.
Of course there is also the upkeep, which is necessary with any machine. Since it is almost always overlooked, degradation happens very fast, transforming spaces, adulterating form and shadow by means of light.
I have yet to visit the Institute of Educational Sciences at Lleida University. I am familiar with the project, have seen pictures of the site, heard some of Siza's complaints (which are, as always, demanding, nonconformist and absorbing), but I am certain that the building is something different and can soon be visited. I would like it if all schools were the same: different.

– Carlos Castanheira

Light from the light cannon illuminates the hallways outside the auditoriums on the ground floor.

Armanda Passos House and Studio
Porto, Portugal
2002–2006

Armanda Passos House and Studio

The house is located on Porto's Avenida do Marechal Gomes da Costa. On this avenue, over time, wealthy families have built villas that express the comfort and the resources enjoyed by their owners. Also on this avenue are located Siza's Serralves Museum and the original Serralves House, which is the largest private property in the city. To the south, in contrast, is one of the city's most established neighbourhoods of social housing. Over the last few years, however, this area has been developed and is changing from social housing to private, upmarket residences.

This house and studio is designed as an artist's work space as well as a dwelling. The building can also be opened up to the public, to become a multi-purpose space. The design of the building, which comprises three interconnected volumes, of which one is separate, gives the three functions of this building a strong relationship, but also allows for a certain independence and privacy for each.

The dominant volume is that of the multi-purpose room, which has direct and almost immediate access from the outside entrance. The function of this ample space can be altered by using the stepping part of its floor level to create a stage. A small hexagonal hall connects with the residence volume. This residence, two storeys high and set back in relation to its urban context, is organized in a relatively traditional way, with the social area on the ground floor and the bedrooms on the upper floor. The studio volume, existing as an annexe, sits on the remainder of the site at the rear and has the usual characteristics of an art studio: high ceilings and large skylights. The store-room and lavatory complete the space and the brief.

Overhanging sun shades that just barely touch allow for sheltered exterior circulation and connection. Within the dwelling and the multi-purpose room, the interior lighting is controlled: sufficient, intimate and varying with the time of day. In the studio, the light is more precise, more penetrating and almost constant.

Inside, the spaces are predominantly white, a white tinted with honey by the oak of the floors. The floors and walls of the bathrooms and lavatories are clad in marble. The exterior walls are plastered in a grey tone that is almost white, or white that is almost grey, depending on the light that plays on the surfaces and angles in an eternal game of form and shadow. The base of the wall is grey granite and has a generous scale. The cornice and other detailing are finished in the same granite stonework. The window and door frames are made of oak clad in stainless steel. The roof finish is zinc.

The garden is part of the project and part of the house. It is a garden that is made up of paved circulation areas, semi-paved sitting areas and green planted areas. The materials, scrupulously chosen, are the same as those used in the building. Some magnificent trees in strategic positions help to define the space. A small granite form, housing air-conditioning machinery, is meticulously placed, and maintains the balance between the three volumes of the house and studio and the boundary wall of the property.

On the avenue where it is located, the house and studio is a villa. Contextually, it stands out due to its introspective form, which makes possible the desired way of living.

– Carlos Castanheira

Sketches studying courtyards
(left) and proportions (right).

Opposite: Aerial view of the building.

Above: Courtyard between the three house buildings.

Building facade seen from the
Avenida do Marechal Gomes da Costa.

211

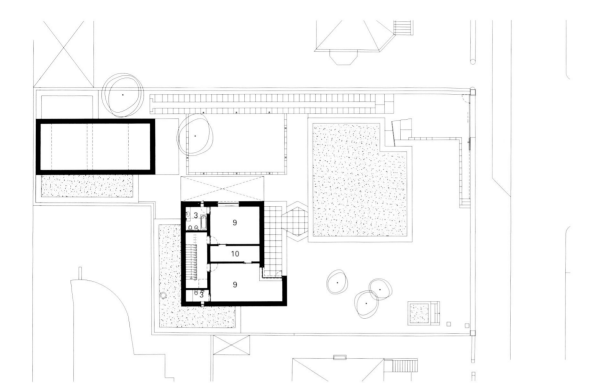

First-floor plan

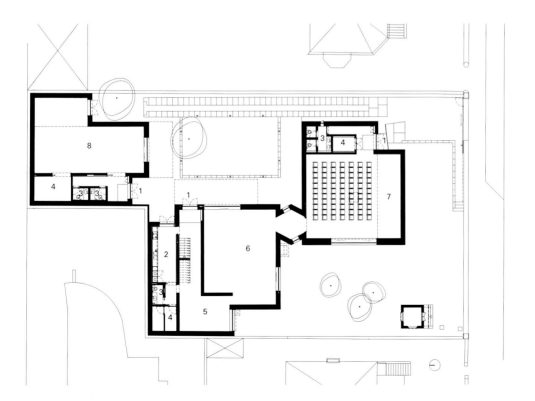

1 Entrance
2 Kitchen
3 Lavatory
4 Storage
5 Snooker
6 Exhibition space
7 Multipurpose room
8 Studio
9 Bedroom
10 Dressing room

Ground-floor plan

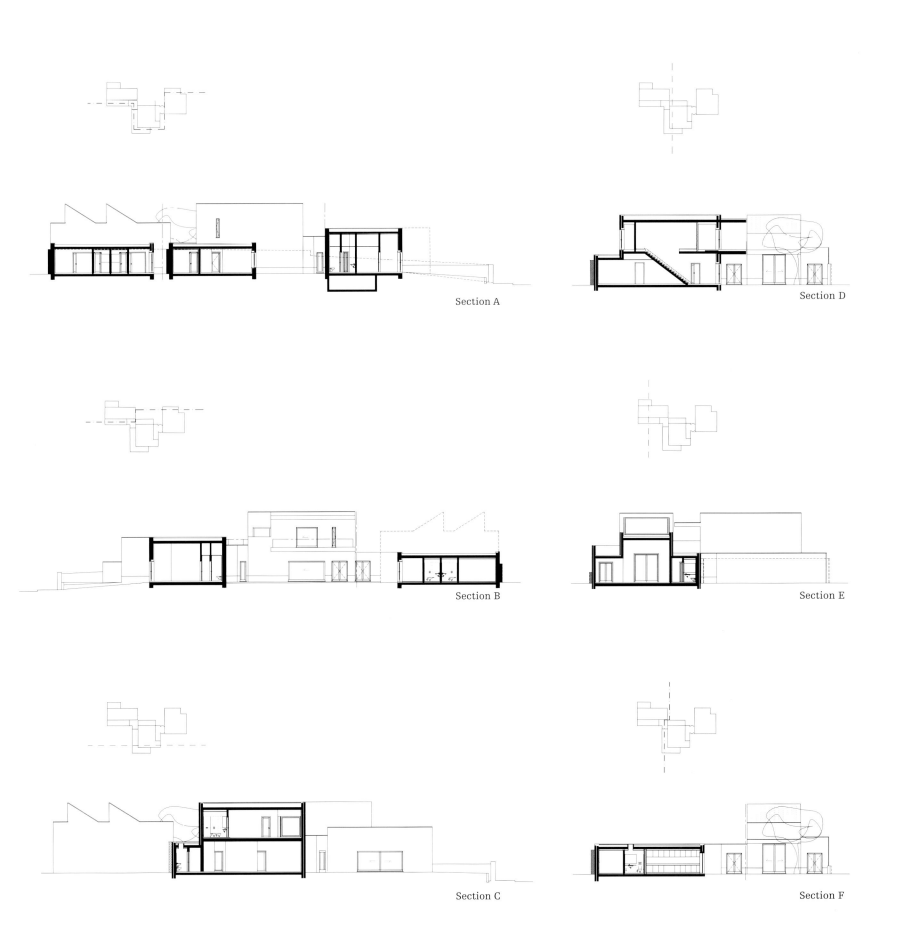

Section A

Section D

Section B

Section E

Section C

Section F

Opposite: Courtyard looking
toward auditorium on the left
and exhibition room on the right
(above) and looking toward
studio (bottom).

Below: Skylit studio space.

215

Centre for Development of New Enterprise
Instituto de Soldadura e Qualidade (ISQ)
Tagus Park, Oeiras, Portugal
2002–2008

Centre for Development of New Enterprise

ISQ's Centre for Development of New Enterprise is situated on a site in Tagus Park. Lying outside the city of Lisbon, beyond a stretch of intensely busy motorway, Tagus Park is an example of a successful business park that primarily houses new generation enterprises. For the first-time visitor, expectations are high, as the success of the programme has been well publicized. On arrival you are confronted by an agglomeration of buildings of diverse architectural style, all contained within what appears to be an intentionally unstructured layout.

The Centre for Development of New Enterprise is reached from the higher level of the site and one is immediately struck by its difference to the rest of the park. This is evident in the order of the architecture, in the distribution of the exterior spaces, in the quality of both the whole and the detail. The centre is housed in two buildings: a main building for offices, laboratories, libraries and lecture rooms; and a smaller building, which comprises an ecumenical centre and gym and sports facilities.

The main building, which has a U-shape, is laid out on four floors. The basement is used for car-parking and technical areas, and access is from the lower-level roadway to the northeast. Above this, a semi-basement is dedicated to new small businesses that require laboratories, with rooms fitted out to suit their different requirements. On each floor, internal circulation follows the perimeter. Shared storage and warehousing spaces are available to the users and similarly there is a meeting room for common use. The internal courtyard formed by the U-shaped layout provides all the laboratories with natural light and ventilation. An external footpath allows direct exit and access to the garden via two stairways located at either end.

The ground floor is the principal access level, and the entrance is located on the eastern side. On entering, visitors are met by the reception, the service areas and the circulation hall. The lavatories are located on the southern side of all floors. The remaining spaces accommodate offices from each of which, where possible, there is access to a large shared veranda, which also acts as a sun break for the lower-level accommodation. This arrangement is repeated on the first floor, which has the same layout as the ground floor but houses smaller offices. Lifts and emergency stairs for vertical circulation to all floors are located at the ends of the building.

The two-storey sports facilities and ecumenical centre is located on the lower part of the site, next to the vehicular access road. On the lower level is situated the sports centre with an indoor pool, male and female changing rooms, a Turkish bath, massage rooms and a gym. An L-shaped, landscaped patio lights and ventilates the internal spaces. On the upper level, with access from the south-facing patio, are located study and meditation rooms, a library and lavatories. A long garden to the north introduces natural light and ventilation as well as inducing calm for meditation or study.

The external landscaping is characterized by two tree-planted car-parks, the stone paving that takes us to the main entrance and the lawn laid over the natural terrain from which the main building emerges. This creates a garden patio between the legs of the U-shape, providing a private and exclusive space for the people who use the building, in contrast to the peripheral space that surrounds the adjoining buildings.

The forms are predominantly white with a render finish. The internal facades of the courtyard are completely glazed, while on the outer facades openings are punched out to establish relationships between the interior and exterior via points of light and to regulate the view of the exterior. Azulino de Cascais stone cladding wraps around the base of the buildings, protecting it, defining hierarchies, and emphasizing the semi-basement level in relation to the broad terrace and the outdoor stairs. The door and window frames are built in bare aluminium and are kept as small as possible, just large enough to perform their functions. Inside, the flooring of the circulation areas is limestone, which at times is continued up the walls in the busier areas. The laboratories and offices, and their access areas, have oak floors. Doors, cupboards and skirting boards are made of painted timber. Walls and ceilings are all painted white.

The same criteria in the use of materials is also applied in the smaller building, so that appropriate materials are used for specialized areas. For example, in the pool area the same limestone used for the rest of the building is applied as flooring whereas the pool itself is clad in blue ceramic tiles.

Although not a daring project – as we have come to expect and ask from Siza – this centre is above all an appropriate project, with everything in its proper place, *comme il faut*, and that's very well. *Comme seul lui sait faire*. A tidy (sound) building, as we agreed on our visit.

– Carlos Castanheira

Opposite above left: Sketch of building form and proportions.
Opposite above right: Sketch of building form in context.
Opposite below: Sketch of building form and entry sequence.

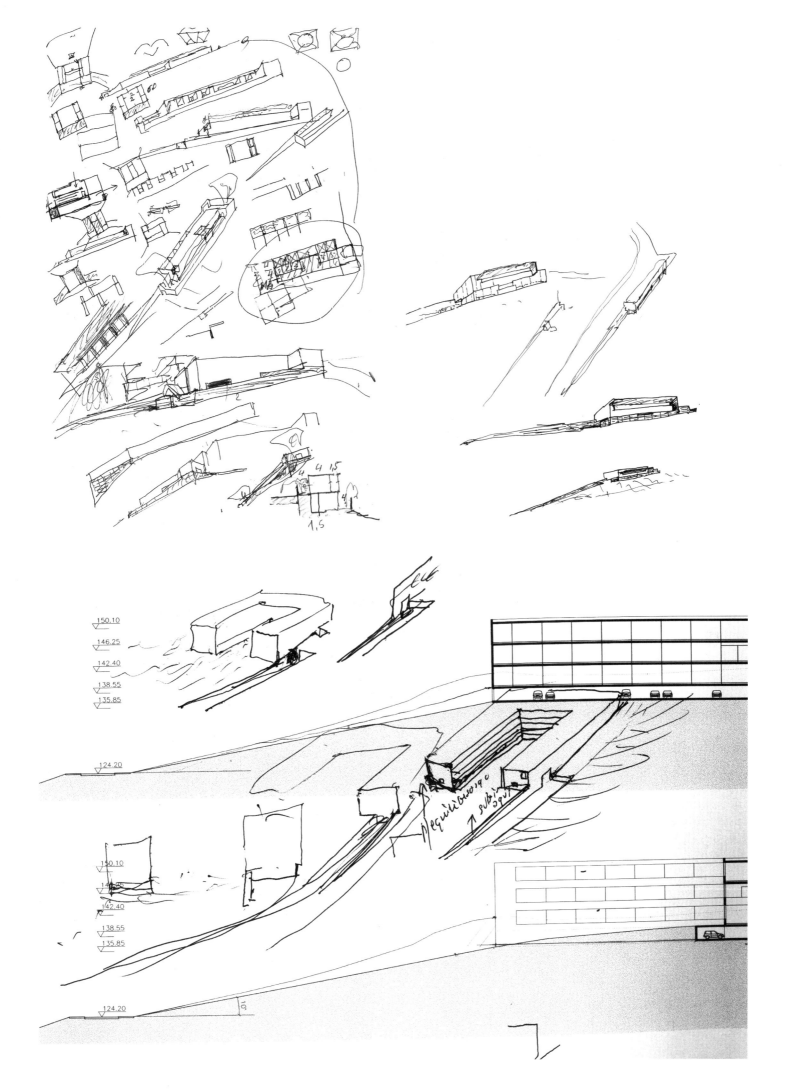

Above: End of south wing

Opposite above: Main entrance to
the office building.
Opposite below: Looking east
past the ecumenical centre
towards the main office building.

First-floor plan

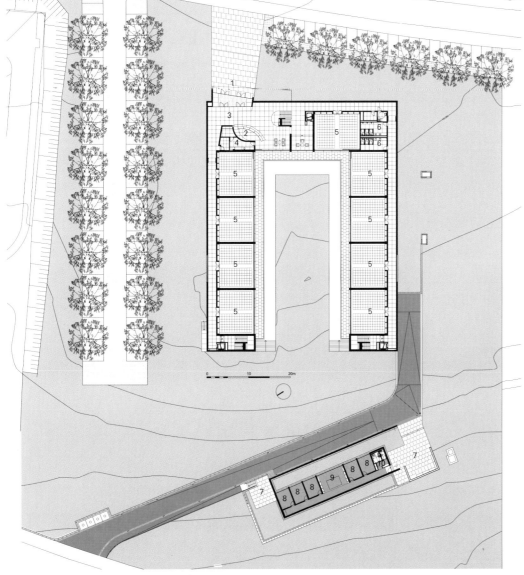

1   Main entrance
2   Reception
3   Atrium
4   Storage
5   Office
6   Lavatory
7   Patio
8   Study room
9   Library
10 Dressing room
11 Equipment room

Ground-floor plan

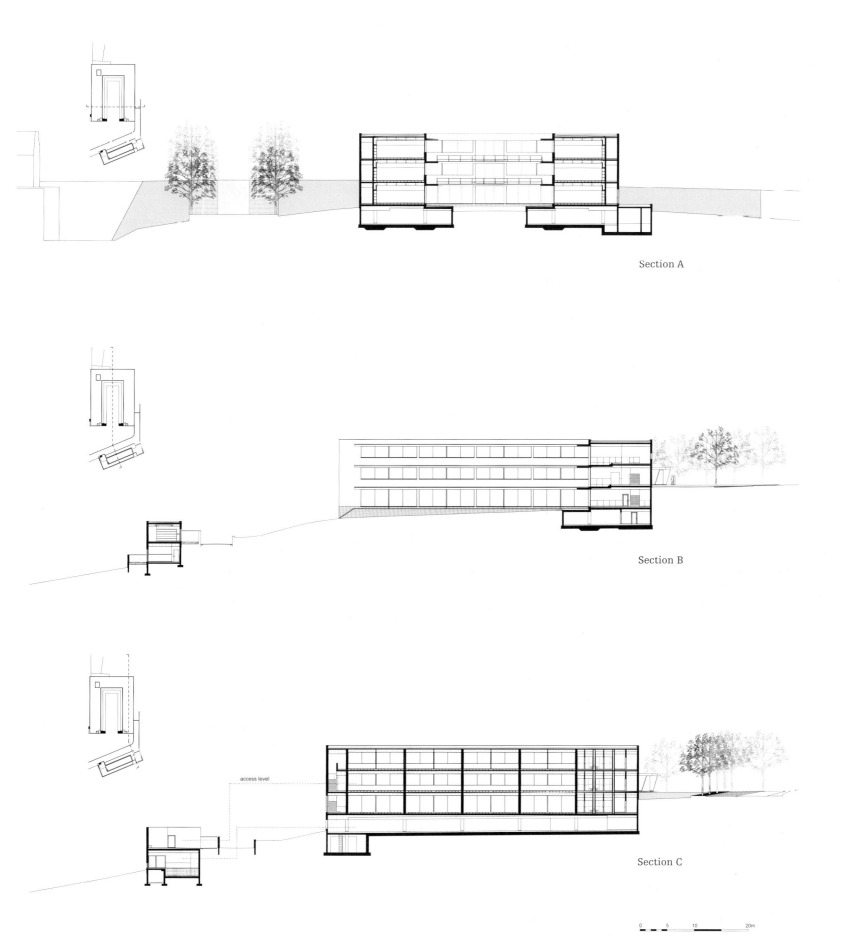

Section A

Section B

access level

Section C

0   5   10   20m

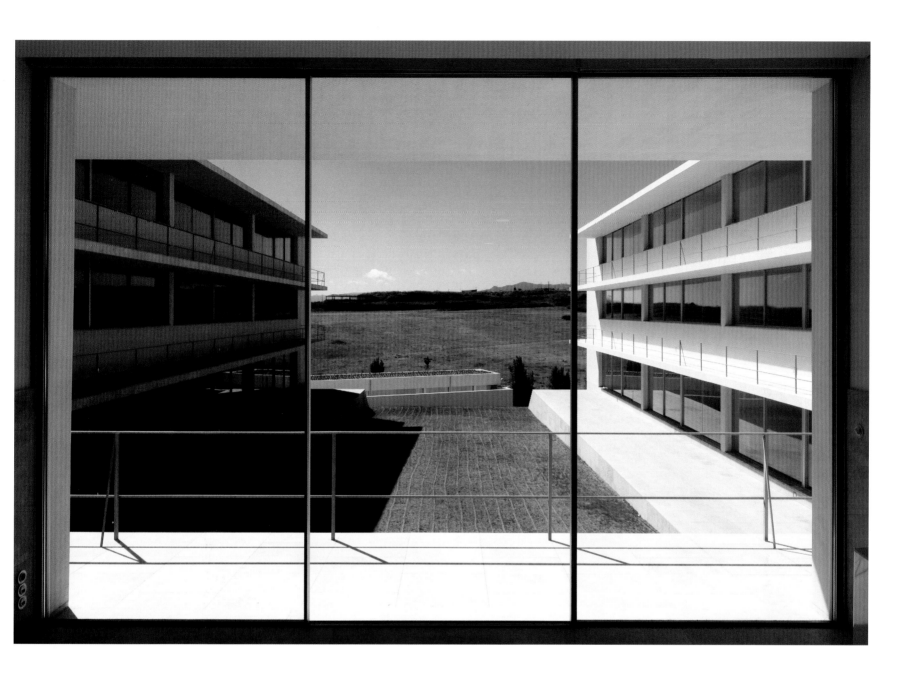

Opposite above: Main courtyard
seen from the west.
Opposite below: Main courtyard
seen from the ground floor of the
main office building.

Above: View looking west from
the east wing of the main office
building.

Above: Looking toward the separate west building, which houses an ecumenical centre.

Opposite above: Staircase near the main entrance in the east wing of the main office building.
Opposite below: Swimming pool, located in the west building underneath the ecumenical centre.

Ribera-Serrallo Sports Complex,
Cornellà de Llobregat, Spain
2003–2006

Ribera-Serrallo Sports Complex

Access to this sports complex is from the northeastern and southeastern ends of the site, via a gently sloping space formed by a multipurpose hall and a long horizontal volume containing the fitness rooms. Through this space, visitors can access the various parts of the programme: the multipurpose hall, swimming pools and fitness rooms.

The multipurpose hall has four spectator stands, one of which is retractable. Spectators enter the hall at its upper level via the principal entrance hallway. A day-to-day entrance for the athletes leads through the same principal entrance hallway and downstairs to the arena level. At this lower level there is a long service block that contains changing rooms. A later phase of construction will include a training pavilion at the end of this block.

To enter the pool area, swimmers descend one level from the principal entrance hallway and arrive at the changing rooms, toilets and saunas. This area is connected to the swimming pools through a gallery that clarifies the separation between the volumes of the pool areas and those of the changing and general service areas of the complex. The public can enter via another gallery at the level of the principal entrance hallway. The fitness rooms and gyms, which have independent access via a vertical circulation core, are distributed along two interconnected levels and share changing rooms with the pool facilities. A provisional car-parking arrangement operates, but is scheduled to be replaced by a permanent one due to be designed in the second phase of works.

– Álvaro Siza

Sketches showing the overall building mass and the interior.

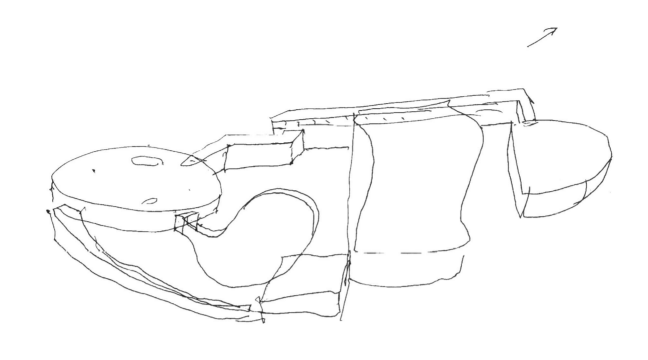

Ribera-Serrallo Sports Complex

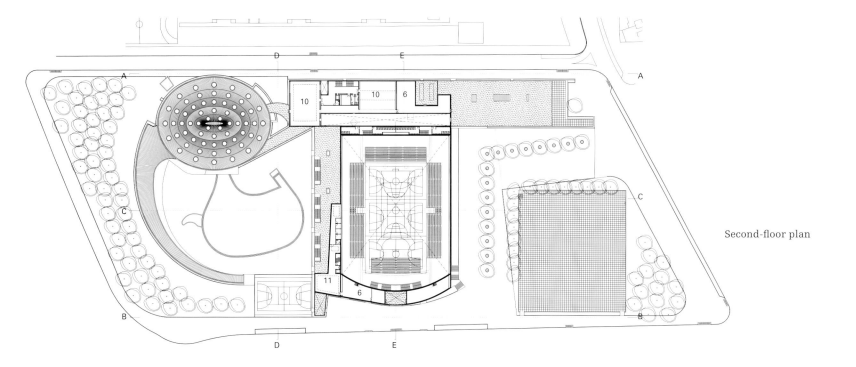

Second-floor plan

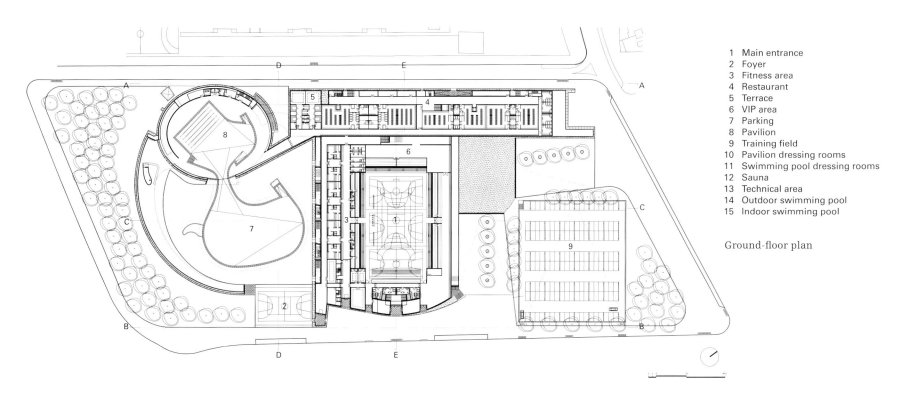

1 Main entrance
2 Foyer
3 Fitness area
4 Restaurant
5 Terrace
6 VIP area
7 Parking
8 Pavilion
9 Training field
10 Pavilion dressing rooms
11 Swimming pool dressing rooms
12 Sauna
13 Technical area
14 Outdoor swimming pool
15 Indoor swimming pool

Ground-floor plan

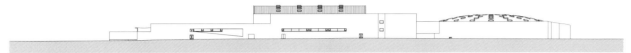

Elevation A

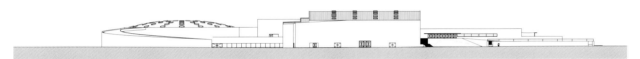

Elevation B

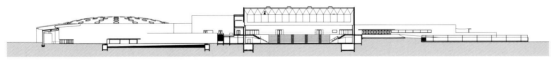

Section C

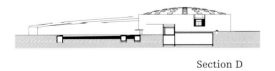

Section D

Section E

Opposite: Division between
interior and exterior pools.　　　Above: Interior swimming pool.

Ramp leading from interior
swimming pool to multipurpose
pavilion.

Silver discs

Out of habit and due to a lack of rigour, we call them 'the swimming pools of Barcelona', although they are not in Barcelona but in Cornellà de Llobregat, and they are not swimming pools but a sports complex.
Cornellà de Llobregat is a town that was once small but has expanded and now forms part of greater Barcelona. It is a peripheral location, and could also easily have been peripheral in its architecture, because it isn't near the historic centre, and the complex was not built for high-profile sports events with media highlights. It is only a sports centre with an area nearly as large as that of the neighbourhood.
The pools are so surprising in their simple beauty that they make us forget the rest of the project. Thus when we want to talk about the whole, we end up talking about the best of it, although the best is, of course, part of the whole, and would not be understandable out of context. The pools are astonishing for their form, or forms, and for the light, the silver discs that move within the indoor pool hall, illuminating and silently transforming the space. It is one of those spaces that can only be understood when visited – its generosity, the quality of its function and the function of its beauty. Will it be allowed to retain its integrity, or will its caretakers introduce the usual glitzy alterations and decorations? The SECIL prize bestowed on it in 2007 has helped to give it the importance and attention it deserves. The exterior is still incomplete and Siza is worried. It seems that there is no money, but something will have to be done. And to do it well will cost the same as to do it badly. Standards must be raised so that the urban environment reaches a high quality.

– Carlos Castanheira

Opposite: Lobby outside the
multipurpose hall. Doors at
the end lead to the ramp down
to the swimming pool.

Below: Interior of
multipurpose hall.

Adega Mayor Winery
Campo Maior, Alentejo, Portugal
2003–2007

Adega Mayor Winery

One only rarely encounters the opportunity to build in a beautiful and untouched landscape and when this does happen, it's a tremendous responsibility. This was the case for this project, where the Nabeiro Group's new winery in Campo Maior lies near but detached from the rest of the industrial complex.

When visiting the site I encountered two fundamental elements that oriented the project and influenced the planting of the building into the landscape: a pre-existing road that united the industrial complex, and a dense clay outcrop, used previously for dumping building rubble, in a cavity excavated specifically for this purpose. There is also a small rocky outcrop in the middle of a wide expanse of gently rolling, cultivated land. The integrity of this natural landscape is reinforced and structured by the agricultural activities that take place there (cork oak plantations and vineyards, also overseen by the Nabeiro Group). These determining elements were complemented by knowledge of the region's architecture.

The winery's rectangular layout, 40 x 120 metres, is based on the existing cavity and constituted by virtually windowless 9-metre-high walls. The cargo and visitors' entrance is located at the southeast end of the building and the volume above it is one storey higher than the rest of the building, providing access to a panoramic roof terrace. The production delivery bay is located at the other end of the building. In between there is a complex production path and a shaded storage area.

– Álvaro Siza

Sketches of the roof terrace and the main entrance.

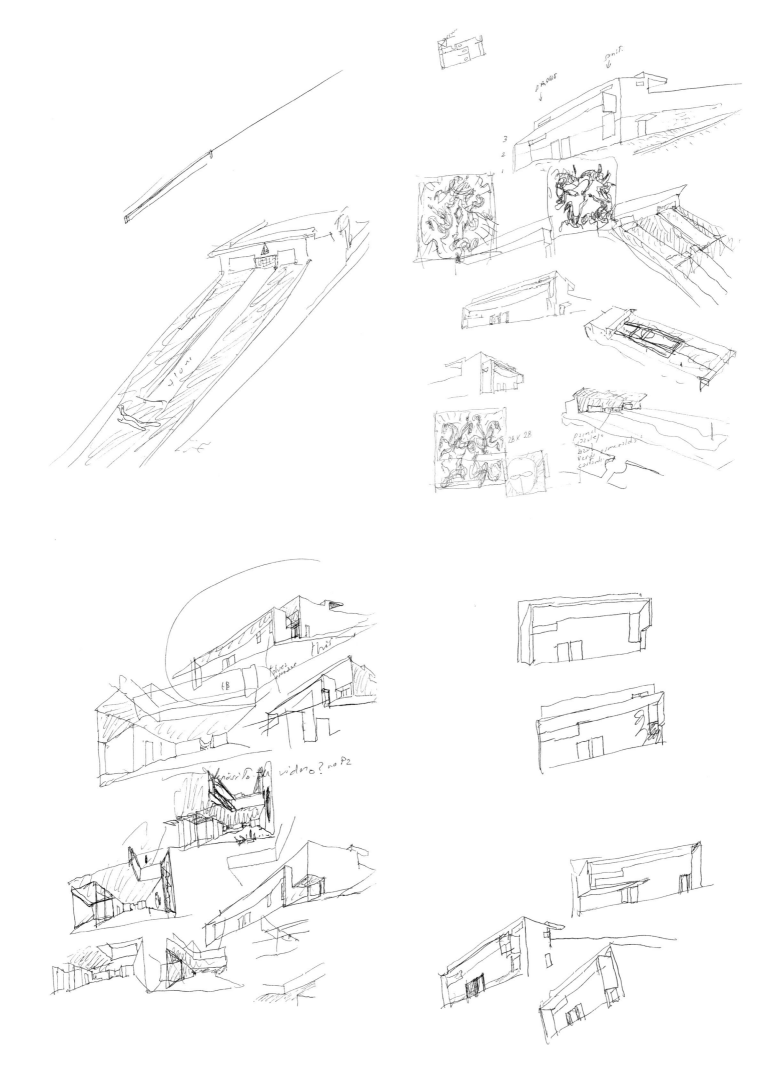

Opposite above: Winery building seen from the vines.
Opposite below: Main entrance, at the southwestern end of the building.

Below: Detail of sun shade at the entry porch.

247

Opposite above: Detail of water
mirror and sun shading on the roof.
Opposite below: Loading dock at
main entrance to the building.

Above: First-floor hallway between
offices and barrel-aging room.

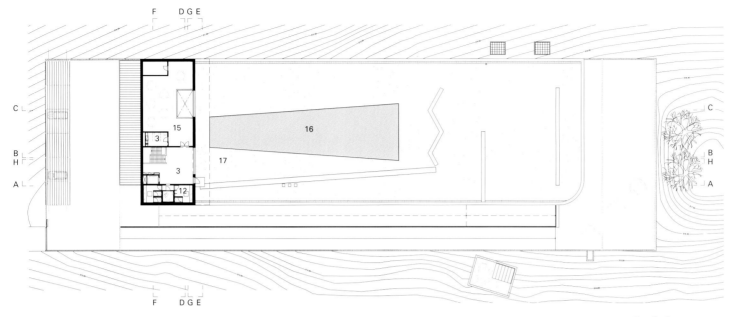

Roof plan

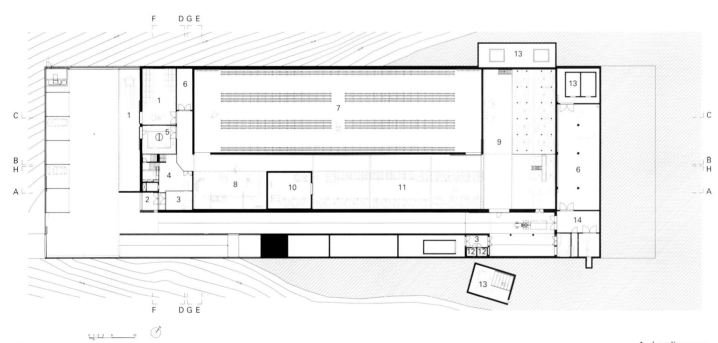

1 Loading area
2 Main entrance
3 Lobby
4 Reception
5 Store
6 Storage
7 Bottle-aging room
8 Bottling and packaging area
9 Red wine fermentation
10 White wine fermentation
11 Wine storage
12 Lavatory
13 Equipment room
14 Communications area
15 Tasting room
16 Water mirror
17 Garden

Ground-floor plan

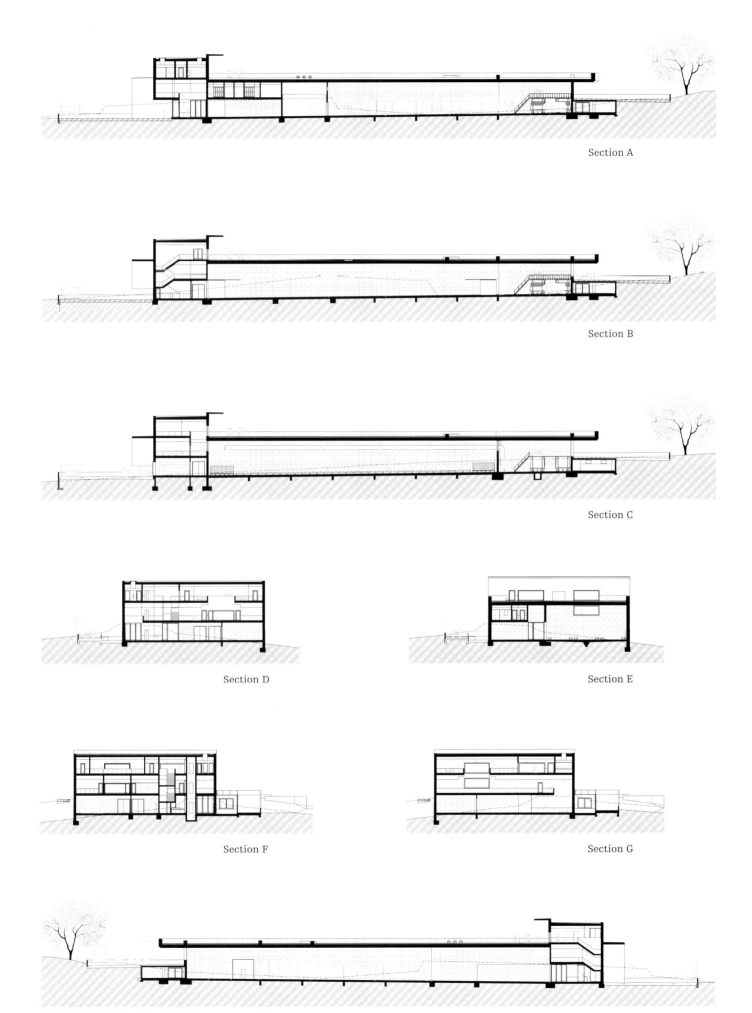

Section A

Section B

Section C

Section D

Section E

Section F

Section G

Section H

A ripple in the flow

To build in an excessively beautiful place is an enormous challenge for an architect, because there is always the danger of destroying it. When the scenery matters (as when because it is 'beautiful and untouched', as Siza puts it in his description) it is difficult to overlay it. Beauty is cruel, and for that reason it does not like competition, or tolerates it only when it is up to its own standards.

In Paul Valéry's dialogue 'Eupalinos, or the Architect', he defines three different types of buildings: some are dumb, some speak and a few sing. The latter type is rare, and he argues that such buildings are the result of both the architect's talent and the Muse's favour. The construction of a winery seems destined to sponsor singing. But such encouragment is insufficient. Indeed, the Muse may have come down, attracted by the alcoholic vapours, but her arrival was not enough. Siza had to add his talent.

And the building of Adega Mayor does sing, and better even than singing to itself or about itself, it sings to the scenery. To use the terms Roland Barthes uses to speak of photography, it registers a *punctum* in the *studium*. For our purposes we can say, it makes a mark in the open fields of the landscape. It lends a key to us with which to read the scenery, or at least to begin reading it, first, of course, by reuniting and assembling its parts, but also by disturbing us, giving us glimpses and surprising us. The building awakens latent forces and introduces new ones. Its merit lies in promoting a balanced tension between the scenic forces of the landscape and those of construction. It does this so well that after it is built, the scenery will not do without the building, nor the building without the scenery, at risk of destroying this newly acquired order.

In the middle of the Alentejo region's landscape, Adega Mayor sings not only due to Bacchus' good auguries, but mostly through Siza's rearrangement of forces, which satisfyingly coordinates scale, orientation, light and shade. He redefines access points and searches for the spirit of the place. The interference with the existing order has created a new one: a meaningful and lasting ripple has been added to the gentle flow of Alentejo's plains.

– Nuno Higino

Barrel-aging room.

Anyang Álvaro Siza Hall
Anyang, South Korea
2005–2006

Anyang Álvaro Siza Hall

This is not Siza's first commission in Korea, but it is his first building to be constructed in Asia. Initially, the objective in organizing the Anyang Public Art Project was to bring together a group of artists and architects and to produce a biennial show of their work. A pavilion was required: a space where it would be possible to show exhibitions, gather together, and that would offer some degree of shelter. It would have to be a simple proposal, without any need for sophisticated equipment or expensive technology, because the budget available would not allow for that. The speedy evolution of the process brought additional requirements to the project and with this design opportunities increased. In addition to the generous multifunctional exhibition space, the following needs were added to the brief during the design process:

– Lavatories for the building's users and for the many tourists who wander around the park where the building is located.
– An independent area for the possible installation of an office for the local police.
– An office for the support and organization of events carried out in the pavilion.
– Air conditioning equipment that would allow the building to be used all year round, rather than only in the summer as had been the first intention.

Despite the commission being originally limited to the design of the building, the project was extended to include the immediate surrounding area.

The building appears as a round form that is equivalent to the perfect surface of a sphere. The organization of the building in plan sets up a hierarchy of spaces while adapting to its locality and emerging from it. The elevation of the walls form various volumes that are separate from the central exhibition space, but together make a single overall volume, a single building.

The principal access is from the public square to the east, through a prominent opening, sheltered by an overhanging roof, linking the outside with the intimate interior. The reading of the interior volume corresponds closely with that of the exterior. The differences are a consequence of the attempt to 'hide' the necessary services, so as to create a space free from any elements that could potentially disturb the tranquillity necessary for art exhibitions, concerts, conferences and other cultural events that will take place there. From the interior it is possible to access the office spaces located on the upper-floor mezzanine, which forms part of the volume further to the west, where the accommodation for the local police is also situated, this being accessible from outside. In the volume to the south, accessed via a narrow covered path, which also allows for circulation around the building, are located the lavatories for men and women, including facilites for users with special needs. All technical equipment is located in a spacious area on the ground floor.

Natural light enters the building through four openings that also create a visual connection with the surrounding area:

– The large opening of the main entrance.
– The opening on to a patio created between the volume of the central space and that of the lavatories block.
– The opening to the south on to a small garden and rocks of a seasonal waterfall, which is shaded by a large overhang to control possible excessive light.
– The opening to the west, with a view of the approach to the entrance, which also serves as a potential emergency exit.

The administration areas have small openings, which just meet building requirements, respecting the hierarchy between the facades and the interior. The west facade, on the ground floor, corresponds to the autonomous space and opens on to the public road with a door and a large glazed area. Above these, two other openings are cut that connect with the administrative areas on the upper floor. Artificial light is supplied by fittings recessed into coving that runs around the rooms, or along the walls in the case of the support areas.

The exterior of the building is finished in an almost-white render, the roofs are zinc and the window frames are made of dark grey aluminium with clear glass. Inside, the walls and ceilings are white, the floor is finished in polished, self-levelling concrete, and the doors, windows and frames are painted wood. A concrete retaining wall, appearing like a tail, exits the lavatory block and extends along the stone retaining wall. On the one hand it enters into a dialogue with it and, on the other, creates limits and gives it a sense of scale.

At the time of the first biennial the pavilion was not completed. It took a little longer for it to be up and running, just in time for its official inauguration. Externally, the building features as a meeting place. Internally, it reinforces the cultural nature of the public square and the park. The space created is both central and centralizing; this can be verified at each biennial, as will surely happen with the second show taking place this year. The building must be treated with care and used with the same attitude in which it was conceived and built.

– Carlos Castanheira

Sketches of the pavilion plan and entrance.

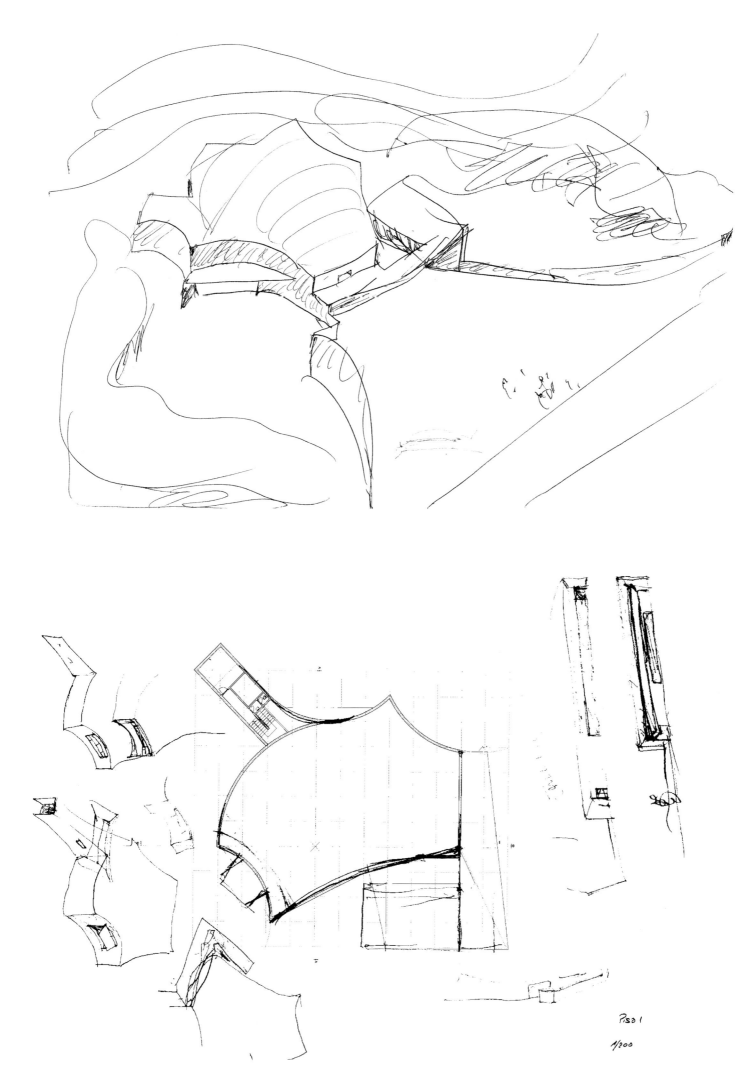

Piso 1

1/200

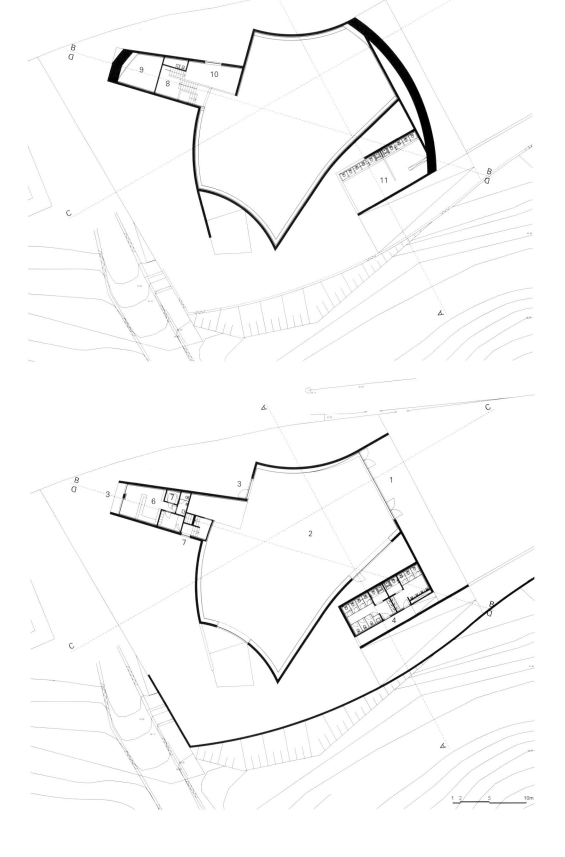

First-floor plan

1   Public entrance
2   Exhibition hall
3   Secondary entrance
4   Lavatory
5   Archive
6   Security point
7   Service entrance
8   Landing
9   Office
10 Meeting room
11 Technical area

Ground-floor plan

Section A

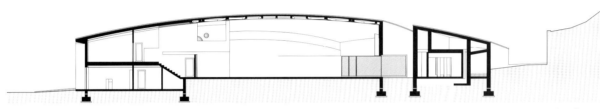

Section B

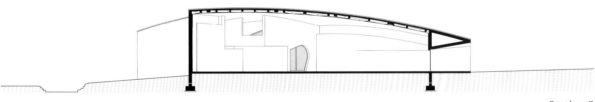

Section C

1 2   5   10m

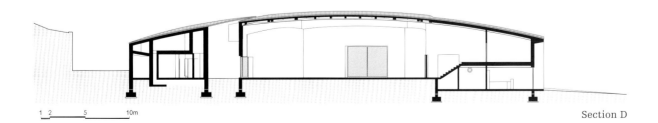

Section D

Anyang Process

In February 2005, we received an invitation, urgent and unexpected. Anyang, a South Korean town of 300,000 inhabitants, was initiating an ambitious programme to become a city of art, starting with APAP2005 – Anyang Public Art Project 2005. A cultural centre was planned for the entrance to a natural park, set among beautiful mountains. Central to the composition, a multifunction pavilion, accessible to all, would be required. Siza was chosen to design the pavilion, and the invitation was hand-delivered to us in Porto.

By March the urgency was real, and I went to the site to survey and accumulate the necessary information for the architect's work. The brief was sparse. It included a multifunctional space, a small office intended for security staff, and lavatories for visitors to the park and the nearby square and restaurants. Jun Saung Kim, a Korean architect who had studied abroad and worked in Porto but was now established in Seoul, was waiting for me on my arrival. We had been friends for over 20 years, and our friendship and common profession created a necessary link.

On arrival, I felt the presence of urgency: the urgency of urgency, so common in Korea, in the people and their lives. There is time to decide, but once the decision is made, urgency begins. There was great euphoria for APAP2005, and many artists and some architects had already confirmed their participation. In addition to the excitement there was also a certain preoccupation: would the invited participants, of so many different nationalities, understand the urgency? In our own time, we began to gather information, take photographs, request maps, and look for documentation. We investigated the architecture that was produced here before its almost complete destruction by the wars, and we identified contemporary architecture of merit. Our friends helped us and showed us examples. The site for the pavilion was an opening in the mountain: a square that was yet to be created, of which we were given half to design. There had already been compromises in the planning, but we tried to get involved and looked for opportunities. We hoped to perhaps even eliminate some of the existing features.

Back in Porto and the West, I tried to transmit the experience, the happenings, the tastes and the background for the work. Siza receives, understands, questions and interprets like no one else. The first work session produced some sketches, still tentative and interpretive. The second session, supported by a site model, became more precise. The form began to take shape with the resolution of the brief. Other sessions followed, typically on Saturdays and Sundays. The atmosphere was great. Models were made, the scale was increased, further sketches indicated changes to the plans, the models and the renderings.

In July, we returned to Korea to make a presentation to the client. On arrival, we were informed that the presentation would be at 5 pm the same day. The meeting included the mayor of the town, relevant councillors and commissioners, council technical staff, local architects and other guests. We presented a selection of Siza's past work, as well as the proposal for the pavilion. After some translation, we were asked searching questions, and given a requirement to increase the size of the public lavatories. This was nothing that would have prevented the formal approval of the proposal, for of course we are technicians and made the necessary changes as requested. We were thanked for the quality of the proposal, but also for our response to the urgency of the situation. The work must be begun, it is necessary to build, it is urgent – and what about the snow? Later that evening, a formal dinner confirmed the client's satisfaction with the project, as well as its acceptance and official approval.

On returning home, we moved on to working drawings. The process was the same but different. The form was adapted to the required small programmatic alterations. The working drawings gained scale and rigour, always following the sketches, which always already anticipated the accuracy required for construction. As the building started, the drawing went on. The internet allowed us to exchange information and to see the structure grow, although at a distance. We took pleasure in seeing the building rise, without the usual bureaucracy, for ours is a different reality.

In November we went back again for the opening of the park and to visit the construction of the pavilion.

The basic volume was complete, completed in grey concrete so fine that it was almost white, allowing us to anticipate the quality of the light. Despite the speed of construction, the execution was perfect. The place was made for this volume and it grew out of the location. In the end, it wasn't possible to change much of the rest of the square, and we were left with our half.

The park was pleasant. What was unpleasant, and a little surprising to me, was the ability to build so much so quickly. Very little was well done, and much of it had a temporary, almost throwaway character. Only the best will last; time is not forgiving. With the client, we discussed infrastructure, services and materials.

We prepared for the next phase, which was the finishes. Back in Porto we followed the completion of the works, almost in real time.

In July 2006, we went back to Korea once again. Despite the exchange of photographs, our surprise was great. Entering the finished space is sublime, as is the light within. The space is not static and, as Siza would put it, when we move, it sings. It is introverted when it needs to be, but extroverted in its perspectives, in its routes, in its volumetric form and in its materials.

It rained and rained; it was the monsoon, which made things a bit dramatic, but presented no real problems. The necessary corrections were few and fundamental, as required in a work by Siza, although we had yet to get to the exterior.

The client – the city – respectfully requested that they name the pavilion the Anyang Álvaro Siza Hall and Siza agreed. As of September 2006, the pavilion was already in use but the inauguration had not yet taken place.

– Carlos Castanheira

Above: Detail of staircase landing opening.

Opposite above: Landing on the staircase to the first floor with openings on to the exhibition hall.
Opposite below: Exhibition hall.

Mimesis Museum
Paju Book City, South Korea
2006–2009

A cat has become a museum

There once was a Chinese emperor who was very fond of cats and it occurred to him to call on the most famous painter in the Chinese empire and ask him to paint a cat. The artist liked the idea and promised that he would work on it. A year passed and the Emperor remembered that the painter had not yet given him the painting of the cat. The Emperor called the artist: 'What about the cat?' 'It's nearly there, it's nearly there!' answered the artist. Another year went by, and another, and another. The scene kept repeating itself. After seven years, the Emperor's patience came to an end, and he sent for the painter. 'What about the cat? Seven years have passed. You promised and promised but I have seen no cat!' The painter grabbed a sheet of rice paper, an ink well, and one of those brushes that only exist in the Far East. With a gesture, elegant and sublime, he drew a cat that was not just a cat but the most beautiful cat ever seen. The Emperor was ecstatic and overwhelmed, and faced with such beauty he did not neglect (which is unusual these days) to ask the artist how much he would charge for such a beautiful drawing. The painter asked for a sum that surprised the Emperor. 'So much money for a drawing that you did in two seconds, in front of me?' said the Emperor. 'Yes, Excellency, that is true, but I have dedicated seven years,' replied the poor painter.

The design for the Mimesis Museum, currently under construction in the new town of Paju Book City in South Korea, is a cat. The client didn't wait for seven years for his design of a cat, but Siza has been designing for more than seven years. Siza has never seen a Korean cat, because he has never been to Korea.

In one day I briefed Siza on the site, showing him a small model to explain the boundaries and the context. In a single gesture, a cat appeared. The Mimesis is a cat. A cat that is curled up but is also stretching and yawning. It's all there; all you need to do is look and look again.

At first the design associates could not understand that this sketch, a cat, could be a building. I have seen many sketches of cats, they always overwhelm me, I never tire of them, I want to see more cats, more sketches of cats, until many times seven years have gone by.

In architecture, after the primary sketch comes the torment. After the initial design, then came models, drawings, corrections to these, then doubts, new drawings, new models, a presentation to the client, who had already seen other projects by Siza, but did not conceal his surprise at this one. The design was approved and the project progressed through the usual steps, which in Korea are shorter and less bureaucratic than those we are used to in the West.

The brief was not altered, but it was, as usual, necessary to make some adjustments due to the development of the design process and the introduction of materials, techniques and infrastructures. We search for representational conventions, so that everyone understands, in an attempt to cover everything.

In the basement we located the archives and the service area, and allowed for an extension to the exhibition area, as has become the habit in museums designed by Siza. On the ground floor are the entrance hall, circulation space, temporary exhibition spaces and a café plus service areas. The administrative and staff areas are located on the mezzanine. The top floor is dedicated to exhibition space.

Light, always light, carefully studied, both natural and artificial, was considered essential to the project, allowing one to see without being seen. We made models and more models, some of which were big enough to enter, and also 3D drawings.

The form of the building is expressed through exposed cast concrete, light grey: the colour of a cat. Inside, there is the white of the Estremoz marble walls and ceilings and the honey colour of the oak. Timber is used for the internal doors and frames, sometimes with glass. Frames facing the exterior are timber and painted steel with crystalline glass.

The building goes on, and so do we; this is how it is in Korea. The project is difficult to build, we worry about the contractor, the various contractors. Our friends and partners are enthusiastic and reassure us.

To draw a cat is really difficult. Try it. It can take seven years. At least!

– Carlos Castanheira

Sketch studies of the central courtyard and building plan.

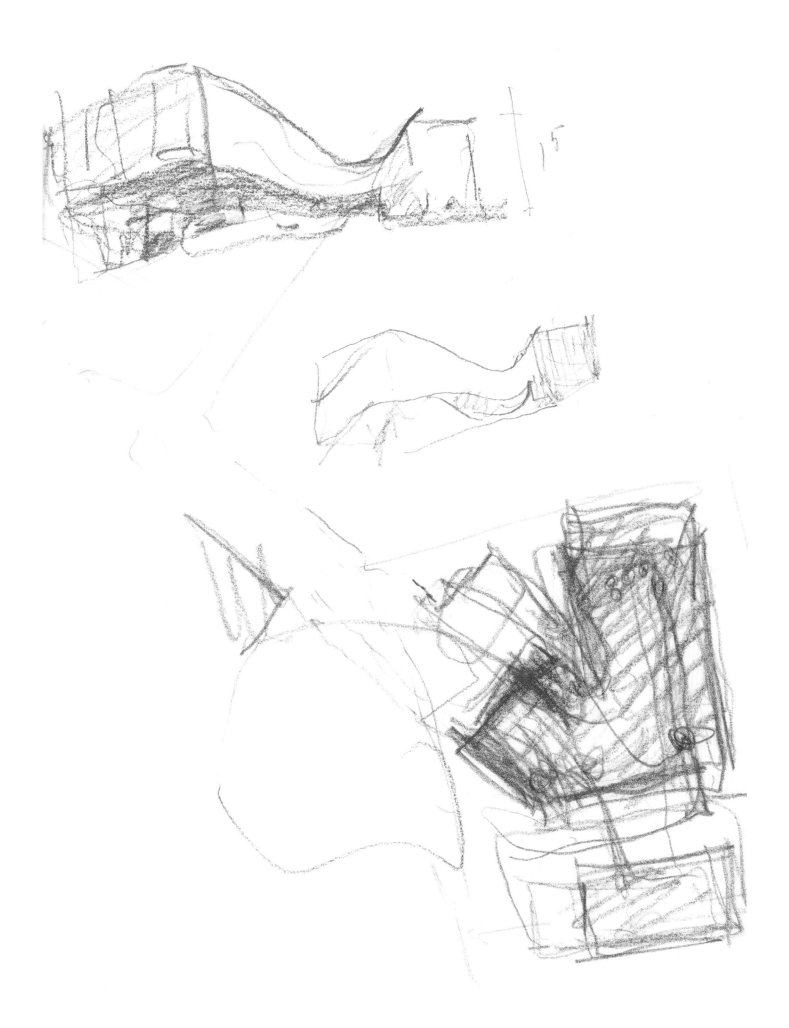

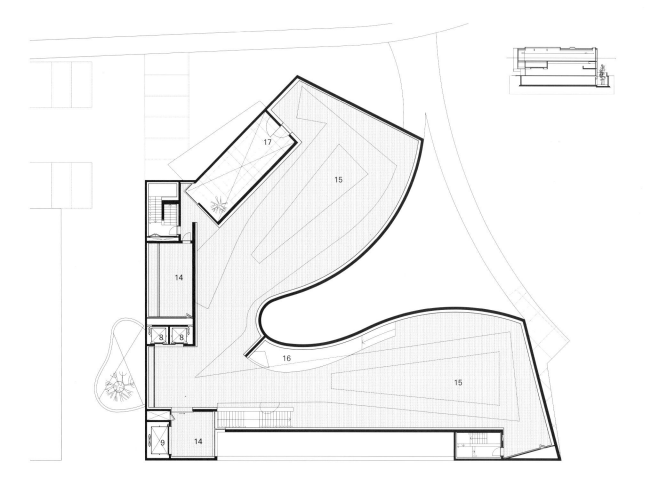

Second-floor plan

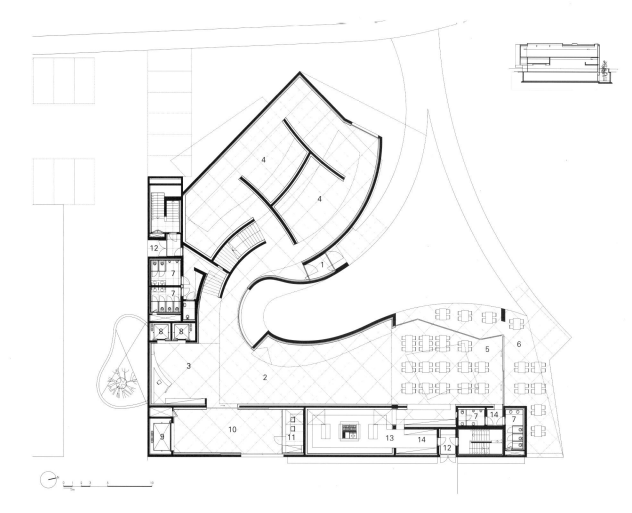

1 Public entrance
2 Foyer
3 Reception
4 Temporary exhibition space
5 Café
6 Terrace
7 Lavatories
8 Public lift
9 Freight lift
10 Loading bay
11 Security point
12 Service entrance
13 Kitchen
14 Storage
15 Permanent exhibition space
16 Exhibition platform
17 Courtyard

Ground-floor plan

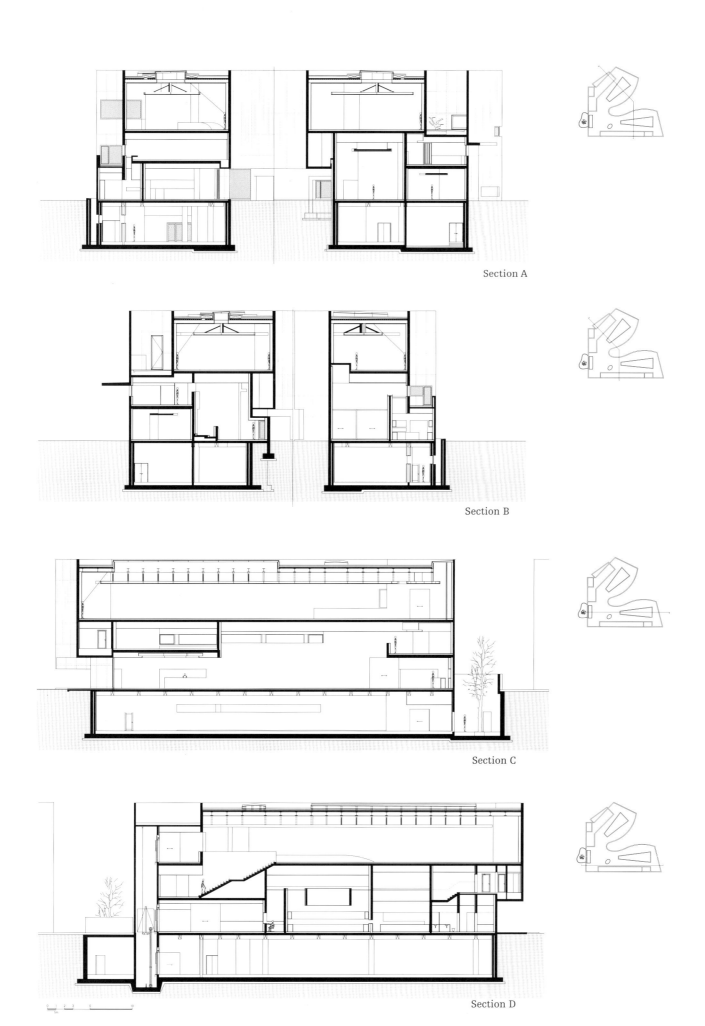

Section A

Section B

Section C

Section D

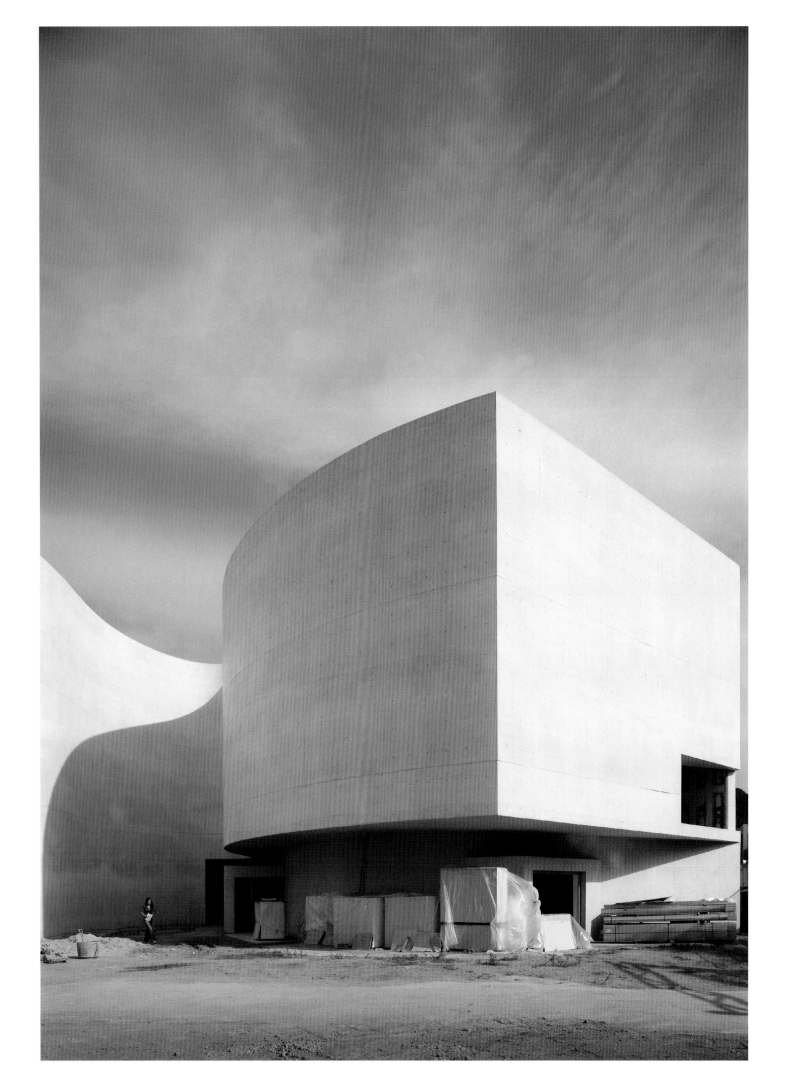

Opposite: West leg of the
U-shape, showing the future
entrance to the museum.

Below: Main courtyard formed
by the U-shape of the building.

277

Mimesis Museum

Quinta do Portal Winery
Celeirós, Sabrosa, Portugal
2006–2008

Quinta do Portal Winery

The new winery of the Quinta do Portal is essentially a store for the ageing and laying down of wines: table wines from the Douro region and Port wines. Beyond its principal function in the process of wine production, the new building must receive visitors, tourists and wine specialists, which means that this facility must be more than a mere place to store barrels and vats.

The rectangular site, of about 24,000 square metres, is an integral part of the Quinta do Portal Estate, one of the largest wine-making investments in the Douro wine region. The entrance, from the public road to the east, allows pedestrian access along a flat platform to the sloping parking area. Positioned 55 metres from the road, the volume of the building integrates into the natural topography of the terrain using a play of volumes and the relationship between access routes and circulation. This arrangement attempts essentially to respond to the functional requirements of both wine storage and the reception of tourists, but it also encourages the surrounding countryside to be absorbed and enjoyed. On arrival we are met by a single-storey volume of rectangular form. Over its roof is a plastic form that contrasts with the volume of the base. As one gets nearer, the base volume gains in dimension, maintaining the cubic and closed impression of a warehouse where sunlight is not often wanted. The upper volume, with its plasticity, is changeable, at times presenting the volume of its forms, at times presenting only a wall.

The materials characterize and accentuate these differences. A base in slate, the local stone, marks the transition between the land, made of stone, and the stone made of earth. Granite is used at the corners and ends, as is always done when it is possible and when one wants to finish something well. Above the slate, light brown walls rise in blocks of recycled cork. The irregular slate is separated from the cork by metal angles and flashings that also establish construction techniques and hierarchies. The colours almost merge; the textures are similar.

Over the materials that form the cellar and characterize its austere function and form, the plastic form dances. The planes of the walls, plastered in an old rose tone, appear both open and closed, at times advancing, at times retreating, letting one see transparencies, suggesting perspectives, imagining curiosities.

If we turn around – it is always necessary to turn around in any of Siza's buildings, as it moves, it is never static, the facades are always different – the single-storey volume turns into an insurmountable fortress. It is easy to imagine that inside something valuable is kept, such as treasure. The volume above the roof moves with us, sometimes hiding itself, sometimes exposing itself, turning the architecture, even the architecture of the store, into something intriguing. One must go in.

In order for the cellar to function efficiently, doors and gates along the service circulation route allow large equipment to pass through. The public entrance is on the arrival plateau. A plastered wall, of the same colour as the upper volume, identifies the way in.

The building is organized over four floors:

– Ground floor: this is almost underground and contains the storage area for table wines, the bottling area, the area for cleaning barrels, a store-room and the staff lavatories.
– First floor: this is the level for deliveries and includes spaces for storing Port wines, the staff changing rooms and bathrooms, and store-rooms.
– Mid-storey: this is the public access level on which are situated the tasting room and servery.
– Second floor: this storey is set back and partially laid out as a landscaped terrace. In this volume is situated the foyer, the auditorium, the projection room and the public lavatories. The terrace, currently being landscaped, represents a kind of repositioning of the terrain occupied by the construction. The landscape viewed from here is always impressive.

The circulation between floors is achieved through a network of staircases that, by virtue of variation and differentiation between arrival and departure points, creates a volumetric and sculpted group within different floors, diversifying them and characterizing them individually.

The interior of the building is generally concrete: walls, floors and ceilings, with structural pillars and joists in steel. The floors in the store and work areas have an epoxy finish. In the public areas some walls are plastered, the ceilings are made of plaster and the floors are finished in oak. In the lavatories and support areas the floors are completed in marble and the walls partially finished in marble or tiles. The external doors and windows are constructed in timber with an exterior finish of stainless-steel cladding.

Vine growing reaches its zenith in the harvest, which takes place over a few days. This is the time of greatest activity in the region. People and machines are mobilized. They eat, drink and harvest. The harvest work is arduous but gratifying: it represents the culmination of a patient process, and wine is the pleasure, earnings and wealth of this region, which is one of the most beautiful in the world. During this period of harvest and abundance, the smells and pleasures of Bacchus transport us to Mount Olympus.

Sketch studies of the staircase leading through the wine production areas.

However, within the Quinta do Portal winery all this activity is not felt, since it is not designed for the diverse phases of winemaking but only for its storage. Here only the best wines will be stored. From here leave masters of the palate. The architecture lends a hand, adding to the pleasures of taste and smell the sensory pleasures of space, form and colour, in a restrained way.

– Carlos Castanheira

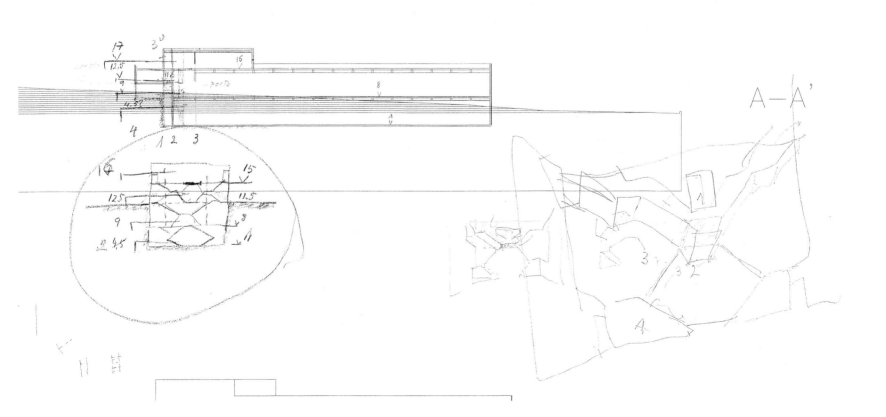

A—A'

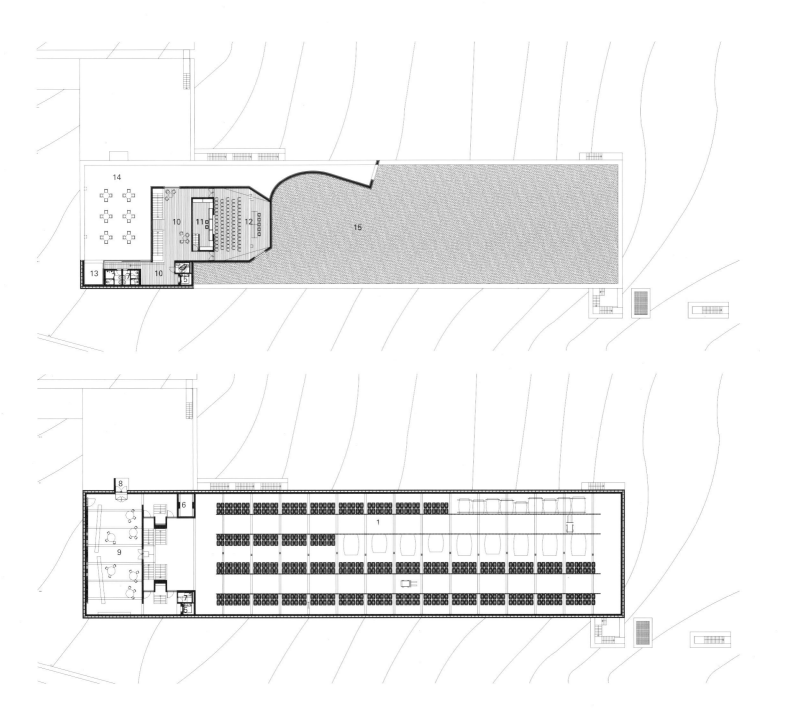

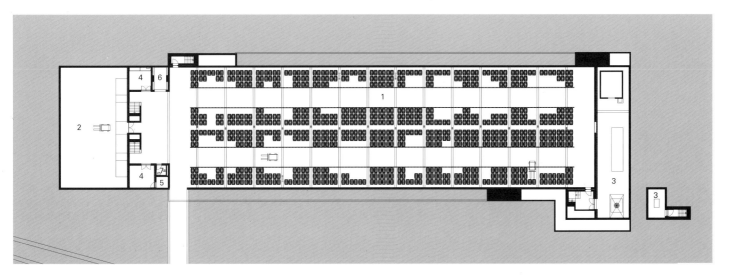

1   Barrel-aging room
2   Bottle storage
3   Equipment room
4   Storage
5   Passenger lift
6   Freight lift
7   Lavatory
8   Main entrance
9   Tasting room
10 Lobby
11 Projection room
12 Auditorium
13 Porch
14 Terrace
15 Roof garden

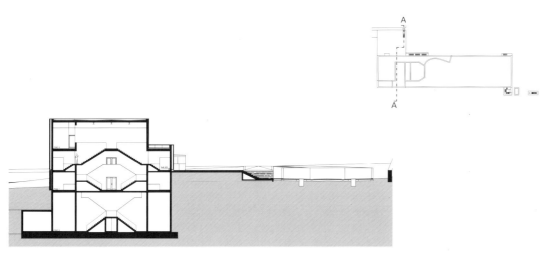

Section A

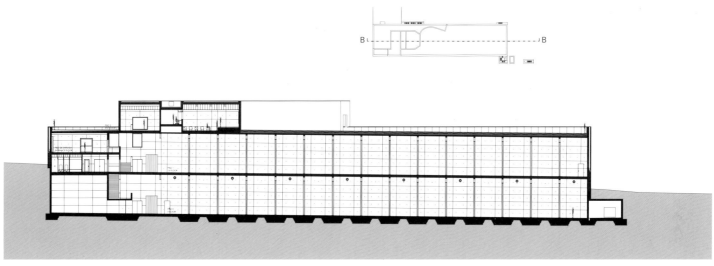

Section B

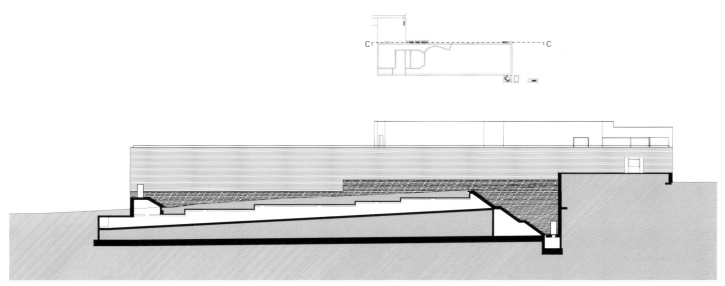

Section C

Opposite: View of the winery
from the northwest.

Below top: View from the
northeast.
Below: Main entrance.

289

View from the roof terrace.

Appendix

Álvaro Siza Biography

Álvaro Joaquim Melo Siza Vieira was born in Matosinhos, near Porto in Portugal, in 1933. He studied architecture at the School of Fine Arts (ESBAP), Porto, between 1949 and 1955, and his first built project dates to 1954. He worked with Professor Fernando Távora between 1955 and 1958. From 1966 to 1969, he taught at the ESBAP, returning in 1976 as Assistant Professor of Construction. He has been a visiting professor at the Polytechnic School of Lausanne, Switzerland, the University of Pennsylvania in the United States, and the School of Los Andes in Bogotá, Colombia. He was the Kenzo Tange Visiting Professor at Harvard University's Graduate School of Design, United States, and he has lectured at the Faculty of Architecture in Porto, Portugal.

In addition to the projects highlighted in this book he is the author of numerous others. In Portugal, these projects include the Boa Nova Tea House and Restaurant in Leça da Palmeira (1958–63), 1200 dwellings for the Malagueira Residential District, Évora (1977–97), the Teacher's Training College in Setúbal (1986–94), the Faculty of Architecture in Porto (1986–96), the library for the University of Aveiro (1988–95), the Serralves Foundation Museum of Contemporary Art in Porto (1991–99), the Church and Parish Centre of Santa Maria in Marco de Canavezes (1990–96), as well as the coordination of the reconstruction of the Chiado area in Lisbon (1988). His projects in the Netherlands include the masterplan for remodelling an area of Schilderswijk in The Hague (1985–89) and three blocks of the Ceramic Terrace complex in Maastricht (1995). In Spain, he has built the Olympic Village Meteorological Centre in Barcelona (1990–92), the Gailician Centre of Contemporary Art (1998–93) and the Faculty of Journalism (1993) in Santiago de Compostela, and the Rectory for the University of Alicante (1995–98). Other completed works of importance include the Portuguese Pavilion for Expo '98, the Portuguese Pavilion for Expo 2000 in Hannover (in collaboration with Eduardo Souto de Moura), the Southern Municipal District Centre of Rosario, Argentina (2002), a Plan of Recovery and Transformation of Cidade Velha, Cape Verde (2000–03), and the Donna Regia Museum of Contemporary Art, Naples, Italy (2005).

Siza has participated in seminars and conferences in Argentina, Austria, Brazil, Canada, Colombia, France, Germany, Greece, Iceland, Italy, Japan, the Netherlands, Norway, Portugal, Romania, Spain, Switzerland, the United Kingdom and the United States.

His works have been exhibited all over the world, including: Copenhagen (1975); Aarhus; Barcelona (1976); Venice Biennale (1978); Milan (1979); Museum of Architecture, Helsinki; Alvar Aalto Museum, Jyväskylä, Finland (1982); Georges Pompidou Centre, Paris (1982); Institute of Contemporary Arts, London; Wonen Foundation, Amsterdam (1983); Technical University, Delft; School of Fine Arts, Porto; Almada Negreiros Gallery, Lisbon (1984); International Building Exhibition, Berlin (1984 and 1987); Massachusetts Institute of Technology, Cambridge (1985); 9H Gallery, London (1986); Columbia University, New York (1987); Harvard Graduate School of Design, Cambridge (1988); Pompidou Centre, Paris; MOPU Gallery/ Ministry of Public Works, Madrid (1990); College of Architecture, Seville (1991); Singel Gallery, Antwerp (1992); Rui Alberto Gallery, Porto; MOPU, Madrid; GA Gallery, Tokyo; São Paulo Biennial (1993); College of Architecture, Granada; College of Architecture, Seville; Sala do Risco Gallery, Lisbon (1994); Galician Centre of Contemporary Art, Santiago de Compostela; Santa Clara Monastery, Republic of San Marino; Ticinese Society of Fine Arts, Mendrisio/Como (1995); Gammel Dok Architecture Center, Copenhagen; Municipal Chamber of Matosinhos; Belém Cultural Centre, Lisbon; and College of Architects, Canary Islands, Tenerife (1996); Architecture Foundation, Brussels (1997); ICO Foundation (Sculptures), Madrid (1998); Basilica Palladiana, Vicenza (1999); Ducal Palace, Venice; Safia Gallery, Barcelona (2000); Art Front Gallery, Tokyo; General Bank, Porto; Artistic and Cultural Association (First Prata Biennial); Lamego (2001); District Archive of Porto; Yokohama Portside Gallery; Art Gallery Atrium, Fukuoka; Bremen City Gallery; Saint-Étienne School of Architecture; Artek, Helsinki; Eighth International Exhibition of Architecture, Venice (2002); Canal Foundation, Madrid; São Paulo Biennial Foundation, São Paulo; Brazilian Museum of Culture; Belém Cultural Centre, Lisbon; UQAM Design Centre, Montreal (2003); Max Protetch Gallery, New York; Architecture Museum, Prague; Ninth International Exhibition of Architecture, Venice; Milan Triennale (2004); Serralves Museum, Porto (2005); Total Museum, Seoul; Santa Monica Museum of Art, California; Southern Centre of Architecture and the City, Toulouse; Cloister of Meritxell Sanctuary, Andorra; Anyang Álvaro Siza Pavilion; Forum of Urbanism and Architecture, Nice (2006); New Delhi (2007); Árvore Cooperative, Porto; Modern Art Museum/Igloo, Bucharest; Gallery L, Seoul, Museum Castromediano / Castello de Acaya, Lecce; Ohtake Institute, São Paulo (2008).

Invited to participate in international competitions, Siza was awarded first prize for the Schlesisches Tor Residential Complex, Kreuzberg, Berlin (1980–84); the recovery of Campo di Marte, Venice (1985); the Remodelling and Extension of the Winkler Casino and Restaurant, Salzburg (1986); La Defensa Cultural Centre, Madrid (with José Paulo Santos) (1988–89); J. Paul Getty Museum, Malibu, California (with Peter Testa) (1993); a study for the Rondanini Pietà Room, Castle Sforzesco, Milan (1999); and a Special Plan for the Prado, Madrid (with Juan Miguel Hernández León and Carlos Riaño) (2002). He also entered competitions for Expo '92 in Seville (with Eduardo Souto de Moura and Adalberto Dias) (1986); A Project for Sienna (with José Paulo Santos) (1988); National Library of France, Paris (with Wilfred Wang) (1989–90); Urban Plan for Brune Boulevard, Cité de la Jeunesse, Paris (1990); Helsinki Museum, Finland (with Eduardo Souto de Moura) (1992–93); Flamenco City, Jerez (with Juan Miguel Hernández León) (2003).

He has won many prizes. The Portuguese Section of the International Association of Art Critics awarded him with the Architecture Prize of the Year in 1982. He was awarded an Architecture Prize by the Association of Portuguese Architects in 1987. In 1988 he received the Gold Medal for Architecture from the Superior Council of the Architecture College of Madrid, the Gold Medal of the Alvar Aalto Foundation, the Prince of Wales Prize from Harvard University and the European Prize for Architecture from the Commission of European Communities / Mies van der Rohe Foundation. In 1992 he was awarded the Pritzker Prize from the Hyatt Foundation of Chicago for the scope of his work. In 1993, he received the National Architecture Prize from the Association of Portuguese Architects. In 1994, he was awarded the Dr. H.P. Berlage Foundation Prize and the Gubbio Prize from the National Association of Historical-Artistic Centres of Italy. In 1995, he won the Gold Medal from the Nara World Architecture Exposition and the International Stone Architecture Prize from the Verona Fair. In 1996, he was given the Secil Prize for Architecture. In 1997, he received the Manuel de la Dehesa Prize from Menéndez Pelayo University. In 1998, he received the Arnold W. Brunner Memorial Prize from the American Academy of Arts and Letters, New York; the IberFAD Prize of Architecture from FAD of Barcelona; the Imperial Prize from the Japan Art Association of Tokyo, and the Gold Medal from the Circle of Fine Arts in Madrid. In 1999, he received the Supreme Cross of the Order of Prince Henry from the President of the Portuguese Republic, and the Leca Construction Prize.

In 2000, the Frate Sole Foundation of Pavia gave him the International Prize of Sacred Architecture. In 2001, he received a prize from the Wolf Foundation in Israel and the Alexandre Herculano National Prize of Architecture. In 2002, he received the Sixth International Compostela/Xunta da Galicia Prize; the Arts Medal from the Arts Council of Madrid, the Golden Lion for best project at the Venice Biennale, the prize for the best architecture career from the Third Ibero-American Architecture Biennial and Civil Engineering in Santiago de Chile, Personality of the Year from the Association of Foreign Press in Lisbon and the Vitruvio Award from the National Museum of Fine Arts, Buenos Aires. In 2003, he received the Medal of Touristic Merit from the Cabinet of the Secretary of Tourism in Lisbon, the 'Palladio d'Oro' from the city of Vicenza and a Distinction of Special Honour from the Official College of Architects of Castilla/La Mancha, in Guadalajara. In 2004, he received the Latin Prize from Union Latina, Lisbon and the Valmor Prize for Architecture from the Municipal Chamber of Lisbon. In 2005, he received the Key to the City from Porto's Municipal Chamber, the Grand Urbanism Prize from the Ministry for Urban Transportation, the Architecture of Granada Prize from the College of Architecture, Granada, a Gold Medal for Cultural Merit and Adopted Son of the City, Santiago de Compostela. In 2007, he received the Secil Prize for Architecture, a Gold Medal and Honorary Citizenship from Matosinhos and a medal of cultural and scientific merit from Marco de Canaveses Town Hall, while the Cultural Ministry of Brazil awarded him with the Order of Merit Cultural. In 2009, he was awarded the 2009 Royal Gold Medal for Architecture from the Royal Institute of British Architects (RIBA).

He has been awarded honorary degrees by the Polytechnic University of Valencia, Spain (1992); Polytechnic School of Lausanne, Switzerland (1993); University of Palermo, Italy (1995); Menéndez Pelayo University, Santander, Spain (1995); National University of Engineering in Lima, Peru (1995); University of Coimbra, Portugal (1997); Lusíada University, Portugal (1999); Federal University of Paraíba, João Pessoa, Brazil (2000); University of Naples Federico II, School of Science and Technology, Italy (2004); University of Architecture and Urbanism 'Ion Mincu', Bucharest, Romania (2005) and University of Pavia Faculty of Engineering (2007).

He is a member of the American Academy of Arts and Science and an Honorary Fellow of the RIBA, the American Institute of Architects (AIA), the Académie d'Architecture de France and of the European Academy of Sciences and Arts.

Appendix

Álvaro Siza's collaborators since 1956

Orlando Varejão, Alexandre Alves Costa, Beatriz Madureira, *António Madureira, Francisco Guedes de Carvalho, Francisco Lucena, Adalberto Dias, Edgar Castro, Nuno Ribeiro Lopes, Miguel Guedes de Carvalho, Eduardo Souto de Moura, Maria Manuela Sambade, Graça Nieto, José Paulo dos Santos, Teresa Fonseca, Bruno Marchand, Jean Gèrard Giorla, Chantal Meysman, Luisa Brandão, *Luisa Penha, *José Luis Carvalho Gomes, Peter Brinkert, Ramiro Gonçalves, Zahra Dolati, Jorge Nuno Monteiro, Mateo Corrales, Roberto Collovà, V. de Pasquale, Oreste Marrone, Viviana Trapani, Anna Alí, Sabina Snozzi, Hughes Grudzinski, Angela Jimenez, André Braga, Susana Afonso, Pier Paolo Mincio, João Pedro Xavier, José Manuel Neves, Helena Torgo, Peter Testa, Pascale de Weck, Carlos Castanheira, Eduardo Marta da Cruz, *Avelino Silva, Luis Filipe Mendes, Humberto Vieira, Tiago Faria, Joan Falgueras, Robert Levit, Alfredo Jorge Ascenção, Mona Trautman, Francisco José Cunha, Joelke Offringa, José Fernando Gonçalves, Christian Gaenshirt, Cristina Guedes, Maria Clara Bastai, *Cristina Ferreirinha, Guilherme Páris Couto, Elisiário Miranda, Jotta Van Groenewoud, Lúcia Peixoto, Luís Cardoso, Antónia Noites, Anton Graf, António Angelillo, João Gomes da Silva, Wilfred Wang, Jun Shuang Kim, John Friedman, José Salgado, Giacomo Borella, Brigitte Fleck, Jan Van de Voort, Jorge Carvalho, Teresa Gonçalves, Salvador Vaz Pinto, Matthew Betmaleck, Ashton Richards, Alessandro D'Amico, Sandra Vivanco, Jane Considine, Yves Stump, *Chiara Porcu, Ana Williamson, *Edite Rosa, João Sabugueiro, Pascale Pacozzi, Cecilia Lau, José Eduardo Rebelo, *Clemente Meneres Semide, Sofia Thenaisie Coelho, Sara Almeida, Carles Muro, Colm Murray, Ulrike Machold, Matthew Becker, Rui Castro, Fariba Sepehrnia, *Miguel Nery, Raffaele Leone, Luís Veiga, Carla Leitão, Margarida Paixão, Joaquim Conceição, Karine Grimaux, Peter Cody, Daria Laurentini, Gonzalo Benavides, Carlos Seoane, Rudolf Finsterwalder, Maria José Araújo, Marco Rampulla, Luis Diaz-Mauriño, Roberto Cremascoli, Daniela Antonucci, Andreia Afonso, Edison Okumura, Paul Scott, Taichi Tomuro, Hana Kassem, Abílio Filipe Mourão, Luís Antas de Barros, Maite Brosa, Maurice Custers, Dirk Sehmsdorf, Madalena Duarte Silva, Rosário Borges de Pinho, Ana Costa e Silva, Susana Correia Leite, Raquel Paulino, Davi Brischi, João Cabeleira, Paulo Sousa, Joana Soares Carneiro, Bárbara Rangel Carvalho, Francesca Montalto, Michele Gigante, Marco Ciaccio, Lia Kidalis, Tatiana Berger, *António Dias, Mariel Suarez, Pedro Rogado, Petra Katarina Alankoja, Francisco Reina Guedes de Carvalho, Vitor Oliveira, Angela Princiotto, Roger Lundeen, Maria Moita, Ueli Krauss, Bradford Kelley, Carolina Albino, Andrea Smaniotto, Filipa Guerreiro, Mitsunori Nakamura, Ameet Sukhthankar, *Atsushi Ueno, *José Carlos Oliveira, Kenji Araya, Benjamin Bancel, Angel Esteve, Antje Kartheus, Nuno Abrantes, Victor Navarro Dias, Axel Baudendistel, Markus Elmiger, Emílio Sanchez Horneros, Verónica Martinez, Gabriel Flórez, *Matthias Heskamp, *Pedro Polónia, Pedro Quintela, Claudia Vogel, Cecilia Alemagna, Tomoko Kawai, Francisco Silvestre, Simon Lanza Olmi, *Hans Ola Boman, Wesley Hindmarch, *António Mota, Paul Nascimento, Laura Menéndez, Saurabh Malpani, Andrea Araguas, Asako Kuribara, *Rita Amaral, *Natacha Viveiros, *Beatriz Tarazona, *Ren Ito, Vânia Miranda, Pablo Elinbaum, *José Pelegrín, *Álvaro Fonseca, *César Escudero, *Naoki Seshimo, Juan Socas, Elisa Martin, Mateo Muro, *Patricia Teixeira, Nicola Natali, Marta Ruiz Cano, *Gonçalo Campelo

Archive/library: Chiara Porcu, Isabel Castro, Rute Gregório
Secretaries: Teresa Godinho, Ivone Sobral, Dinora Rodrigues, *Anabela Monteiro, *Maria João Sousa, Manuela Andrade

* Current collaborators

Credits

Bouça, Águas Férreas Cooperative
Porto, Portugal
1973–1978 / 2000–2006

1st Phase
Design: 1973–76
Construction: 1977–78
Client: Association of the Inhabitants of Bouça
Architect: Álvaro Siza
Collaborators: António Madureira, Francisco Guedes de Carvalho, Adalberto Dias, Miguel Guedes de Carvalho, Eduardo Souto da Moura, Maria Manuela Sambade, Nuno Ribeiro Lopes, José Paulo dos Santos
Consultants: João Araújo Sobreira (structural); Jorge Malta (electrical installation and equipment)

2nd Phase
Design: 2000–03 / Construction: 2004–06
Client: Águas Férreas Cooperative
Architects: Álvaro Siza and António Madureira
Collaborators: Rosário Borges de Pinho, Raquel Paulino, João Cabeleira, Paulo Sousa, Ana Costa e Silva
Consultants: GOP–João Maria Sobreira (structural); GOP–Raquel Fernandes (water and plumbing); GPIC–Alexandre Martins and Raul Serafim Costa (electrical and safety); GET–Raul Bessa (HVAC)
Text: Álvaro Siza, September 2006; Nuno Higino, May 2007

Bragança Terraces
Lisbon, Portugal
1992–2004

Client: Imopólis SA
Architect: Álvaro Siza
Coordinators: Clemente Meneres (1st Phase), Miguel Nery (2nd Phase)
Collaborators: Ashton Richards, Francesca Montallo, Cláudia Vogel, Cristina Ferreirinha, Vítor Oliveira, Michele Gigante, Maria Moita, Mitaunori Nakamura, Atsushi Ueno, Tomoko Kawai
Consultants: STA–António Segadães Tavares (structural); STA–António Vieira Pereira (electrical); STA–Carlos Palma (mechanical, hydraulics and gas); João Gomes da Silva (landscape architecture)
Text: Álvaro Siza, February 1999; Carlos Castanheira, May 2002

Insel-Hombroich Foundation Museum of Architecture
Hombroich, Germany
1995–2008

Client: Insel-Hombroich Foundation
Architect: Álvaro Siza with Rudolf Finsterwalder
Consultant: Horst Kappauf
Text: Carlos Castanheira, October 2008

São Bento Underground Station
Porto, Portugal
1997–2005

Client: Metro do Porto
Architect: Álvaro Siza
Coordinator: Clemente Meneres Semide
Collaborators: José Carlos Oliveira, Atsushi Ueno
Consultants: Balfour Beatty Company / EFACEC (electrical and mechanical)
Text: Carlos Castanheira, May 2007; Nuno Higino, May 2007

Zaida Building, Patio House
Granada, Spain
1993–2006

Architect: Álvaro Siza
Construction director: Juan Domingo Santos
Project coordinator: Ola Boman
Collaborators: Luís Dias, Peter Testa, Edison Okumura, Francisco Silvestre, Emílio Horneros
Consultants: GOP–Jorge Silva (structural); GOP–Raquel Fernandes, Alexandre Santos (hydraulics); Higini Arau (acoustical); Alexandre Martins, Fernando Aires (electrical and safety); GET–Raul Bessa (HVAC)
Text: Álvaro Siza, March 1995; Carlos Castanheira, May 2007

Iberê Camargo Museum
Porto Alegre, Brazil
1998–2008

Client: Ibère Camargo Foundation
Architect: Álvaro Siza
Building coordinator: Josè Luis Canal
General consultant: Pedro Simch
Coordinators: Bárbara Rangel (1st Phase), Pedro Polónia (2nd Phase)
Collaborators: Michele Gigante, Francesca Montalto, Atsushi Ueno, Rita Amaral
Consultants: GOP–Nunes da Silva (Structural); GET–Raul Bessa (HVAC); Raul Serafim, Alexandre Martins (electrical); GOP–Raquel Fernandes (hydraulics); GOP–Higini Arau (acoustical)
Text: Álvaro Siza, August 2004

Centre for 'Camilian' Studies
Vila Nova de Famalicão, Portugal
1998–2005

Client: Vila Nova de Famalicão municipal council
Architect: Álvaro Siza with Luisa Penha
Construction assistance: José Luís Carvalho Gomes
Consultants: GOP–João Maria Sobreira (structural); GOP–Raquel Fernandes (hydraulics); GET–Raul Bessa (HVAC); GPIC–Alexandre Martins (electrical); Maria Rosa Sá Ribeiro (acoustical); João Gomes Silva (landscape architecture)
Text: Álvaro Siza, May 2005; Nuno Higino, May 2007

Multipurpose Pavilion
Gondomar, Portugal
2001–2007

Client: Gondomar
municipal council
Architect: Álvaro Siza
Licence and technical assistance:
António Mota (1st Phase),
José Pelegrin (2nd Phase)
Collaborators: Cristina
Ferreirinha, Juan Socas, Mateo
Muro, Gonçalo Campelo.
Construction direction: Sara
Matias, Jorge Leal
Consultants: João Maria
Sobreira (structural); Alexandre
Martins, Fernando Aires
(electrical); Raul Bessa (HVAC);
Raquel Fernandes, Alexandre
Santos (hydraulics); Philip Newel,
Sérgio Castro (acoustical);
Dimas Pinto (sporting facilities)
Text: Álvaro Siza, June 2001;
Nuno Higino, May 2007

**Masterplan for Vila do Conde's
coastal road**
Vila do Conde, Portugal
2001–2007

Client: Vila do Conde
municipal council
Architect: Álvaro Siza
Collaborators: Marco Rampulla,
Barbara Rangel, Benjamim
Bancel, António Mota, Antje
Kartheus, Francisco R. Guedes
(1st Phase), Kenji Araya, Ola
Boman (2nd Phase)
Consultants: GOP–João Maria
Sobreira (structural); GOP–
Raquel Fernandes, Alexandre
Santos (hydraulics); GPIC–
Alexandre Martins (electrical);
GET–Raul Bessa, Costa
Pereira (HVAC); Pedro Melo
(agronomy); Álvaro Raimundo
(surveying and budget)
Text: Álvaro Siza, January 2001;
Nuno Higino, May 2007

Municipal Library
Viana do Castelo, Portugal
2001–2007

Client: Viana do Castelo
municipal council
Architect: Álvaro Siza
Collaborators: Edison Okumura,
Maria Moita, Francisco Reina
Guedes, Tatiana Berger,
Verónica Martinez
Construction coordinators:
Tatiana Berger (1st Phase), José
Manuel Pelegrin (2nd Phase)
Consultants: GOP–João Maria
Sobreira (structural); GOP–
Alexandre Martins (HVAC);
GET–Raul Bessa (electrical,
communication and fire); GOP–
Raquel Fernandes (hydraulics);
José Manuel Pelegrin (furniture
and outdoor urbanization)
Text: Álvaro Siza, July 2005;
Nuno Higino, May 2007

**Masterplan for Leça da
Palmeira's coastal road**
Matosinhos, Portugal
2002–2007

Client: Matosinhos
municipal council
Architect: Álvaro Siza and
António Madureira
Collaborators: João Cabeleira,
Rosário Borges Pinho, Raquel
Paulino, Paulo Sousa
Consultants IDOM–António
Almeida (special); Helena Isabel
M. Ferreira (surveying)
Contractor: Tecnifeira
Text: Álvaro Siza, May 2003;
Nuno Higino, May 2007

House in Pego
Sintra, Portugal
2002–2007

Client: Carlos Alemão
Architect: Álvaro Siza with
António Madureira
Construction director:
Carlos Alemão
Collaborators: João Cabeleira,
Rosário Borges Pinho, Raquel
Paulino, Paulo Sousa
Consultants: GOP–Jorge Nunes
da Silva (structural)
Text: Álvaro Siza, January 2002;
Carlos Castanheira, May 2007

House in Mallorca
Palma de Mallorca, Spain
2002–2007

Architect: Álvaro Siza
Coordinator: Atsushi Ueno
Construction coordinators:
Rafael Moranta and
Miguel Capllonch
Consultants: GOP–Jorge Silva,
Raquel Dias (structural); GOP–
Raquel Fernandes (hydraulics);
GOP–Raul Serafim, Alexandre
Martins (electrical); GET–Raul
Bessa (HVAC)
Text: Álvaro Siza, May 2007;
Nuno Higino, May 2007

**Institute of Educational
Sciences**
Campus de Camppot,
University of Lleida
Lleida, Spain
2002–2008

Client: University of Lleida
Architect: Álvaro Siza with
Manuel Somoza
Associated office: ARESTA,
Arquitectura + urbanisme:
Manuel Somoza y
Manel Glez Solanes
Collaborators: Beatriz
Tarazona, Laura Menédez,
Verónica Martinez, Emilio,
Sanches Horneros
Consultants: GOP–Jorge Nunes
da Silva (structural); Raul Bessa
(HVAC); Raquel Fernandes
(hydraulics); Alexandre
Martins (electrical and fire);
Raul Serafim (electrical)
Text: Álvaro Siza, May 2007;
Carlos Castanheira, May 2007

**Armanda Passos House and
Studio**
Porto, Portugal
2002–2006

Client: Armanda Passos
Architect: Álvaro Siza
Coordinator: Simon Lanza Olmi
Consultants: GOP–Jorge Nunes
da Silva (structural); GPIC–
Alexandre Martins (electrical);
GET–Raul Bessa (HVAC); GOP–
Raquel Fernandes (mechanical);
Text: Carlos Castanheira,
October 2008

**Centre for Development of New
Enterprise**
Tagus Park, Oeiras, Portugal
2002–2008

Client: ISQ–Centre for
Development of New Enterprise
Architect: Álvaro Siza
Contractor: Teixeira Duarte
Collaborators: Claudia Vogel
(preliminary project), Natacha
Viveiros (built project)
Consultants: GOP–Jorge Nunes
da Silva (structural); GPIC–
Alexandre Martins (electrical);
GOP–Raquel Fernandes
(mechanical); GET–Raul
Bessa (HVAC)
Text: Carlos Castanheira,
October 2008

Ribera-Serrallo Sports Complex
Cornellà de Llobregat, Spain
2003–2006

Client: Cornellà de Llobregat
municipal council
Architect: Álvaro Siza
Coordinators: Marco Rampulla
(1st Phase), José Manuel
Pelegrin (2nd Phase)
Collaborators: Markus Elminger,
Gabriel Flórez, Atsushi Ueno,
Pedro Polónia
Construction director:
Luís Fullola
Consultants; Jorge Nunes da
Silva (structural); Alexandre
Martins, Raul Serafim, Fernando
Areias (electrical); Costa Pereira,
Raul Bessa (mechanical); Raquel
Fernandes, Fernanda Valente
(hydraulics); Manuel Somoza
(measuring); Dimas Pinto (sports
facilities); Higini Arau (acoustics)
Text: Álvaro Siza, November 2006;
Carlos Castanheira, May 2007

Adega Mayor Winery
Campo Maior, Portugal
2003–2007

Client: Nabeiro Group
Architect: Álvaro Siza
Coordinator: Avelino Silva
Collaborator: Rita Amaral
Consultants: GOP–João Maria
Sobreira (structural); GOP–
Alexandre Martins (electrical);
GET–Raul Bessa (HVAC); GOP–
Raquel Fernandes (hydraulics);
GOP–Eng. Alexandre Martins
(security); Álvaro Siza 2–
Arquitectura Lda. (landscape)
Text: Álvaro Siza, January 2005;
Nuno Higino, April 2007

Anyang Álvaro Siza Hall
2005–2006
Yong-il Park, Anyang, South
Korea

Client: Anyang municipal council
Architect: Álvaro Siza with
Carlos Castanheira and
Jun Saung Kim
Collaborators: Orlando Sousa,
Demis Lopes, Bruno André, João
Figueiredo, Seungwook Kim,
Dusuk Jang
Consultants: TNI Structure
Engineering (structural);
JUNG–Mioung Engineering
Group Co., Ltd. (electrical)
Text: Carlos Castanheira,
September 2006 (Anyang
process); October 2008
(Project description)

Mimesis Museum
Paju Book City, South Korea
2006–2009

Client: Open Books
Architect: Álvaro Siza with
Carlos Castanheira and
Jun Saung Kim
Collaborators: Dalila Gomes,
João Figueiredo, Youngil Park,
Chungheon Han
Consultants: Jung-Myung
Engineering Group Co., Hansan
Engineering Co., Jungang
Construction Engineering
Consultant, Hanool Construction
Text: Carlos Castanheira,
May 2007

Quinta do Portal Winery
Duoro, Duoro Region, Portugal
2006–2008

Client: Sociedade da
Quinta do Portal
Architect: Álvaro Siza
Collaborators: Gabriel
Florez (preliminary project),
Gonçalo Campello
Project coordinator:
Pedro Polónia
Construction coordinator:
Miguel Nery
Consultants: GOP–Jorge Nunes
do Silva, Valeriy Shongin, Ana
Silva (structural); GET–Raul
Bessa, Miguel Alves (HVAC); GPIC
–Alexandre Martins (electrical);
GOP–Raquel Fernandes,
Alexandre Santos (mechanical)
Text: Carlos Castanheira,
October 2008

Index
Figures in italics refer to illustration captions

Phaidon Press Limited
Regent's Wharf
All Saints Street
London N1 9PA

Phaidon Press Inc.
180 Varick Street
New York, NY 10014

www.phaidon.com

First published 2009
© 2009 Phaidon Press Limited

ISBN 978 0 7148 4946 1

A CIP catalogue record for this book is available from
the British Library.

Designed by Joost Grootens
Printed in China

All photographs are by Fernando Guerra – FG+SG.

Texts were translated by Jane Considine and Tiago Faria.

The author would like to address a special word of thanks
to: Álvaro Siza, Anabela Monteiro, António Madureira,
Avelino Silva, Atsushi Ueno, Beatriz Tarazona, Chiara
Porcu, Fernando Guerra, Jane Considine, João Figueiredo,
José Pelegrín, Luísa Penha, Matthias Heskamp, Miguel
Nery, Natacha Viveiros, Nuno Higino, Pedro Polónia,
Rudolf Finsterwalder, Sérgio Guerra, and Tiago Faria.

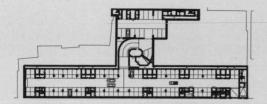
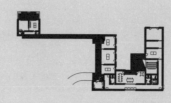
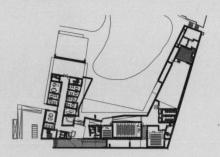

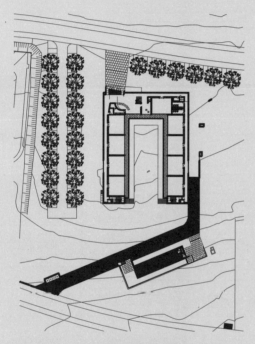
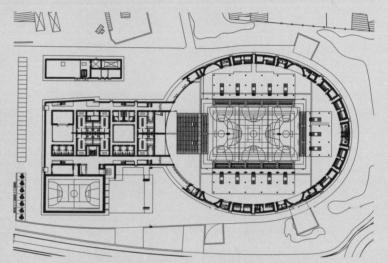
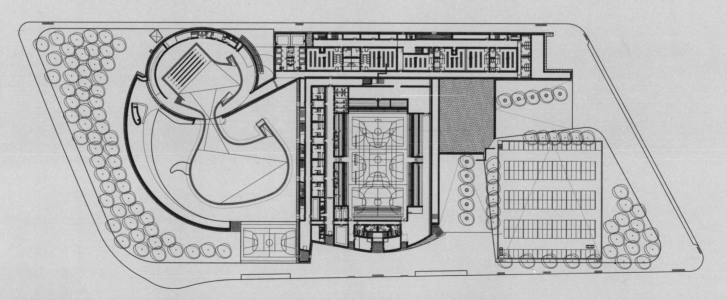